THE CHURCH,

THE CITY

&

THE VIRUS

WHERE WAS THE CHURCH?

THE CHURCH,

THE CITY

&

THE VIRUS

WHERE WAS THE CHURCH?

ISBN 978-0-6208824-2-2

'May all who come behind us find us faithful [1]'

Dedicated to all those leaders who labour diligently in the service
of under resourced organisations, serving under
resourced communities all over the world.

REVIEWS

Trevor Herbert is an exceptional leader and leader of leaders. If you are passionate about transformation I wholeheartedly recommend you read his book 'The Church, The City & The Virus'"

Matt Bird
CEO of Cinnamon Network International

- - - - 0 - - - -

Thank you to Trevor, by the Grace of God, for the decision to write: "The Church, The City & The Virus" and for allowing the Spirit to guide and lead him. The reflections and observations are evidently coming from someone with a deep love for the Church.

He creatively uses confrontation: the gift nobody wants in a questioning process to bring out the truth about the collapse of church culture as we know it, not because of Covid 19. The book exposes the kind of church we have become. I will advise you to grab yourself a copy!

Mbulelo Bikwani
Executive Director: Sucgrate Consulting Services (Pty) Ltd
Chairman, Western Cape Ecumenical Network (WCEN)

- - - - 0 - - - -

We watch the statistics of Covid-19. How many died and how many lives were affected. Trevor Herbert went beyond that. He paused to ask questions. Probing and uneasy questions. Disturbing questions. Trevor actually mentioned the C word. C-corona, C-Covid19. Not only that, he critiqued the C word and gave it a context. But there is also a downside to this book.The nature of its context and content presupposes a sequel. We are left wondering how the work, witness and ministry of the church will look in a post Covid19 world.

Bruce Theron
Director: Ekklesia
Faculty of Theology, Stellenbosch University

- - - - 0 - - - -

This is an honest look at the Covid-19 / coronavirus pandemic that has impacted us here in South Africa, from the viewpoint of a church leader, based on his exposure to and understanding of the situation.

After my reading of this work, it might be appreciated why I would recommend a study of this account for further discussion and debate amongst church leaders who would love to see the transformation of their cities.

Barry Isaacs
Director of: Three-cord Family Foundation
Chairman: Cape Town for Jesus (CT4J)

- - - - 0 - - - -

The author brilliantly documents the journey, highlighting the spiritual and social nuances that played out as the church has navigated the COVID-19 pandemic so far. He captures succinctly how secular governments marginalised and disregarded the Church in relegating it to the level of a social event, with regulations more stringent than even that relating to the taxi industry.

He places fair blame on the church for capitulating and cowering to the powers that be, never raising their voice. The impact on the rural and township church is eye-opening - This reaffirms the reality that we are deeply unaware, not only of the critical role that the church plays within disadvantaged communities, but the devastating impact the regulations have had on those vital spiritual communities.

Alan Platt
Global Leader Doxa Deo / City Changers

- - - - 0 - - - -

In this book, Trevor Herbert asks some difficult questions regarding the decisions surrounding our nation's response to the Covid-19 epidemic. Was Covid -19 an opportunity for the body of Christ to positively live out Jesus' command or was it simply an interruption to the daily activities that keep us busy? The Great Commission was not a request or suggestion but rather a command that we should GO into all the world, making disciples of every nation.

I believe this included a Covid infected world. Like Trevor, I choose to believe that Africa has both the potential and the opportunity to be salt and light to a disillusioned world. 2020 will come to an end, the pandemic will be contained and history will judge the impact that the Church had, or did not have, on both the victims and the spread of the virus in our cities and nations. Difficult times require difficult decisions and actions. It is my prayer that we will not be weighed in God's scale and be found wanting, because we never acted boldly, spoke out, or prayed fervently enough.

Graham Power
Chairman: Power Group
Founder of the Global Day of Prayer and Unashamedly Ethical

- - - - 0 - - - -

None of us has been here before!

That is the case with the global and relentlessly unfolding Covid-19 pandemic that we in 2020 find ourselves in.We are all learning as we move forward! In this captivating account, Trevor Herbert, a colleague in Movement Day Africa has sought to share early lessons with us. Notable is his vivid sharing of his frustration as he seeks to engage with leaders in his own city, his church denomination and the broader Church. His agony comes through as he ponders the church's silence that in his review finds 'herself' at the end of the line!

The message from his real life current leadership experiences is clear: Whether you lead from the front, side, centre or behind, when the challenge appears, its indispensable for the leader to take to the front, for the moment clearly visible and casting a bold posture.
Trevor's agony as a leader is not unique; similar deafening silence is rife across the continent; that he has captured this so quickly and

plainly and voiced it in his engagements and in writing for posterity is unique - and in itself a present leadership lesson in the backdrop of the Coronavirus!

Stephen Mbogo
International CEO
African Enterprise / Lausanne Africa (EPSA) Regional Director

ACKNOWLEDGEMENTS

This book was completed during an extraordinarily difficult period in the history of our city, our country and the world. Much lies behind us and much lies ahead of us. May God help all of us and grant us clear direction, wisdom and insight for the rest of the journey.

In the first place, I am deeply grateful to my Creator for bestowing on me so much grace that I might be allowed to serve the Church of our Lord Jesus Christ and His people in so many ways and in so many places. As the song says, 'there are so many others with greater distinction that He might have chosen'.

Secondly, to my wife, children and grandchildren, thank you for giving to me, over so many years, such an incredible environment to live and work in. During the last two decades of my life, most of my work hours have been from home - and what a lovely place to call home - thanks to all of you.

Thirdly, I would like to express my most profound gratitude to my beloved Church, the Apostolic Faith Mission of South Africa (AFM of SA) for the lifelong opportunity to serve the church since my teenage years. So much of what I have learned about life and leadership I have learned here.

Fourthly, please allow me to say thank you to those who have contributed in one way or another towards this work, especially Dr Mac Pier of movement.org, New York, for so graciously agreeing to write the foreword and all those who have honoured this work with their comments and reviews.

Fifthly and finally, to all those leaders and organisations where I have had the God given privilege to learn and grow (and continue to do so) - thank you so much for tolerating me with all my shortcomings and imperfections. Many of you have taught me so much about living a life of humility and service.

PREFACE

'Whatever your hand finds to do, do it with your might…'
Ecclesiastes 9:10a (New King James Version)

When I started writing this book during the month of May 2019, I had in mind putting down my thoughts in writing about the challenges the contemporary Church was facing in an ever-changing society, in particular the way the world's cities was changing. I even had a working title in mind for the book, *The Church and the City*. After about a year, not much had been written yet and amid my very busy diary, finishing what I had started before the winter of 2020 would arrive, was not really at the top of my agenda. However, something happened that changed all that complacency and between the months of March and May 2020, I found myself writing with a new urgency. Here is the result.

An avid reader myself, my personal preference is for a book that has some substance, but one that is not too long. Of the few thousand books in my personal library, very few have been read right through, and if any, then only those with less than 150 pages. Having said that, I express the hope that whoever may find the time and the inclination to read this work, will find some substance within its pages and, in addition, find it readable and not too long. The primary audience I hope to reach are leaders, especially church leaders. However, like any writer, I suppose, the wider the audience that responds to the book, the greater the compliment to the author. Therefore, I hope that not only leaders will find the content useful.

It is not the first time I have written a book, but neither am I a prolific writer. Truth be told, this is only my second book in more than 25 years and the first was, probably, for a much wider audience. The title of that work was *Affirmative Action in the South African Workplace* [2]. As the title may suggest, that book was a response to the direction that was being taken by the leaders of our new democracy as far as the democratisation of the workplace was concerned. This time the circumstances in the external environment has again prompted me to write, albeit about a very different scenario from more than a quarter century ago. The addition to my working title of a year ago (*and the virus*), hopefully explains enough in this regard.

As was the case with my first work, my approach is to say what I believe needs to be said - as clearly and as concisely as I can. I honestly hope that I have been successful as far as that is concerned. The Bible teaches us to speak the 'truth in love' and right through the book, I have tried to remain mindful of this. There was no desire on my part to speak the brutal truth and if it may come across like that in some of the pages, please believe me that it was not intentional. However, wherever the reader observes the repeated emphasis of what I believe to be the disregarded facts, for that emphasis, respectfully, I believe no apology is necessary.

While a number of critical observations of the current South African situation are made in this work, I believe that I have gone out of my way to avoid any direct or personal attack on any individual holding any office. On the contrary, it is perhaps necessary, right at the outset, to make this much clear. I have the greatest respect and admiration for the president of my country and for the leaders of my own denomination, as well as those leaders with whom I serve in other organisations. In most instances anyway, what may be perceived as criticism within these pages, is not about what was done by anybody, but about what, in my view, was not done.

This period, from March to May 2020, has in all probability, been one of the most difficult that our nation, and the rest of the world, has ever endured. Moreover, as everybody is continually reminding us, the worst is yet to come. The learning curve has been huge - for all of us. None of us has all the answers, but I am of the firm belief that all of us have a duty to make our contribution towards the eradication of this new invisible enemy that has encroached on our territory. The duty to speak when those who are in the influential position to do so are silent, should not be neglected either. Especially when it appears as if the silence amongst those who should have spoken has been caused by the paralysis of division within their own ranks.

Trevor Herbert
Cape Town, South Africa

Pentecost Sunday, 31 May 2020.

FOREWORD

Trevor Herbert has provided us with an extraordinarily important book of self-reflection. The globe and Africa have been experiencing the twin trauma of the COVID 19 pandemic and more recently unsettling race relations. His book has invited us into an important conversation. Having been to Africa every year from 2002 – 2019, I have seen the extraordinary progress of the gospel across the continent.

The book is important for three reasons. First, the reflection is on the context of Africa and in particular Cape Town, South Africa. Africa is the part of the world where there is perhaps the greatest concentration of agony and opportunity for the gospel anywhere. The average African is ten years younger than the average person on every continent in the world. I believe that sub Saharan Africa and Europe are the two great global battle grounds between the two major world religions. Understanding the context of Africa is critically important.

Historically many of the great early church fathers are African – Augustine, Tertullian, and Origen to name a few. During the burning of Rome, Augustine famously said, "The City of God is not the City of Rome. It is both invisible and imperishable." It is important to have Augustine's perspective during these difficult and uncertain days.

Herbert's call is similar to that of the church fathers in the first century – to care for the poor and the widows even at great risk to ourselves. Christianity grew 800 times in 300 years from 25,000 to 20 million adherents because of the selflessness of the church in the major urban centres of the first three centuries.

Secondly – the call is to have a critical understanding of our communities and cities. Our behaviour must be rooted in the role of the church in specific ways addressing our most vulnerable. Herbert describes with great chronological detail what has been unfolding in his own city and nation during the pandemic. Demographics matter. We need to know where our most vulnerable are and how we can best serve them to secure their basic needs for survival. The South African church has played such an historically critical role in journeying through apartheid into freedom and providing leadership to the globe in uniting the church for the larger cause of the gospel.

Herbert's final admonition is to lead. We are in a critical moment not unlike the first century where the first disciples knew that the furtherance of the gospel was more important than the longevity of their own lives. Africa has so many vulnerable populations. This is a sovereign moment where the Church can lead locally and partner globally to change the trajectory of so many multitudes of people across the continent. Leaders do what leadership requires. What happens in Africa will alter the trajectory of 21st century Christianity as much as any other region of the world.

Dr Mac Pier
Founder, movement.org, New York, USA

TABLE OF CONTENTS

INTRODUCTION

'I'm telling you what I'm telling everyone: Be alert!'
Mark 13:37 (International Standard Version)

We would all be new at this. Inexperienced. Mistakes were going to be made.

The Church was getting ready for something. But not for this. For the longest time now, the Church has been questioned and challenged about its relevance in an ever-changing world and society. On an increasing scale, the so-called millennials were seeking their spiritual food in other contexts. To keep them interested in church life and church activities was becoming one of the most pressing priorities for the Church. Not only for the millennials. Everyone else was finding so much else to do on Sunday mornings. There were so many attractions and distractions. Many church leaders were experiencing a sense of inadequacy in their abilities to perform their duties and live out their calling and vocation.

It was most certainly not for a lack of trying. Church leaders were going out of their way to get their axes sharpened and to get themselves better equipped for the new day that was dawning. Their annual diaries filled with leadership seminars and conferences - at home and abroad. Staying abreast of developments in all the aspects of ministry like contemporary worship, hospitality ministry as well as developing better preaching skills and techniques were all part of a day's work. Not only trying to get people into church, but, at the same time, trying to get the believers out of church and into the marketplace where they could be salt and light in their places of work and beyond.

Believers all over the world were being encouraged to become more aware of their surroundings - their communities and their cities. Of the needs and habits of the people around them and how they (the believers) could add value to the lives of those individuals in need of hope, reassurance and direction. The Church was preparing herself to become more than only spiritually vibrant. Much more than that, she (the Church) was also seeking to become culturally relevant and more socio-economically involved. The recent research about how the Church was doing globally, in terms of growth in attendance and membership, was also very encouraging. The Church, it seemed, was not a dying institution after all.

Speaking of research, the Church was using this tool to great effect. With organisations like that of the Barna Group, Pew Research Centre and the South African company, Consulta, it was now possible to gain an understanding of the behaviour and preferences of different age groups, city dwellers compared to rural folk, how to respond to the needs of people within multi-cultural settings as opposed to mono-cultural settings and so on. All over the world, para-church organisations were burgeoning. In particular, a type called gospel city movements - organisations focused on cities, life in the city, how the world's cities are changing and how the Church should be ready to respond to the worldwide exodus from the rural areas of the planet to the cities of the globe.

The common global challenges facing the planet was not far from the agenda of the Church. Together with other stakeholders, the worldwide Church was involved in collaborative efforts to understand and interpret the latest urban trends with a view to be in a state of greater readiness to respond to the ever-changing environment outside the stained glass windows of the Church. Poverty, unemployment and inequality, amongst others, were no strangers to

2

the Church or her members. To tell the truth, in so many cases, wherever there was pain, loss and brokenness it was the Church and her servants who, in most cases, would be first on the scene, long before governments, politicians and business people.

Did I say, state of greater readiness? Yes, the global Church was not exactly idle when she celebrated Christmas at the end of the year 2019. She was getting ready for something. Ready to make a more meaningful contribution to the world she was in. Ready to collaborate with other organisations and leaders with more or less similar objectives as the Church, including leaders responsible for the management and wellbeing of cities and their citizens. This was nothing new. All over the world, there were numerous examples of how the Church and other stakeholders had already taken hands and were making a noticeable difference in the lives of the communities whom they served. However, while we were still rinsing off the dishes after Christmas lunch, something was already happening on the other side of the world.

Something, it seemed, the Church was not ready for.

Chapter 1
THE UNSTOPPABLE OUTBREAK

*'The thief does not come except to steal, and to kill, and to destroy.
I have come that they may have life, and that they
may have it more abundantly.'*
John 10:10 (New King James version)

'We are not trying to stop this outbreak from coming; we are trying to stop it from coming quickly.[3]'

These are the words of Professor Dale Fisher, chairperson of the Global Outbreak Alert and Response Network of the World Health Organisation (WHO). Time will tell if that objective, as expressed by the good professor, was achieved and if, indeed, the decisions and actions of the WHO contributed to the successful slowing down of the ruthless advancement of the novel coronavirus, or if the other alternative (of simply allowing the virus to take its course) would have been too ghastly to even contemplate.[4] This new outbreak would, for months to come, in almost all the local and international news media become the world's number one news item. In all probability, never before in the known history of the human race would something so catastrophic play out before our very eyes.

Nevertheless, long before the arrival of the coronavirus and COVID-19, planet earth was already dealing with a myriad of other challenges - from hunger and homelessness, to global warming and pollution, as well as the so-called fourth industrial revolution, amongst many other things. The list is endless. Here in South Africa, one may often hear of the evil triplets - poverty, inequality and unemployment. However, what are the common global challenges[5] and how ready are the world's cities to deal with these? As far as world health was concerned, people were dying by the millions from many other diseases besides the fatal effects of COVID-19 for the longest time. Even during the height of the pandemic, not nearly as many were dying due to COVID-19 as were dying from many other killer diseases.

According to the World Health Organisation, heart disease and stroke cause more than half of the deaths worldwide. Other leading causes of death in the world are chronic obstructive pulmonary disease, lung cancer, diabetes and dementia. These are the top five killers, in a manner of speaking. Besides these top five, yet more diseases were causing many more deaths than the novel coronavirus. Nevertheless, during the year 2020 COVID-19 went right to the top of the list of challenges facing the world and it seemed that it would remain for some time to come.

Depending on who responds to the question of what the list of the world's top challenges might look like, the answers may vary. It seems to be a moving target. However, there are common challenges facing humanity that most experts and agencies agree on. For starters, there is the growing gap between the rich and the poor and the consequences that flow from that. This ever-widening gap feeds the vicious cycle of poverty and lack of access to basic items like food, shelter, education, employment and healthcare.

Secondly, there is the aspect of sustainable development and the balancing act of providing for the growing population of the world without unduly depleting the natural resources of the planet. Add to this the impact of climate change on the availability of water resources and the subsequent access to enough clean water for both city dwellers and rural communities. One of the world's top tourist destinations, the city of Cape Town in South Africa, in recent times have experienced its worst drought in one hundred years, and the continued threat of drought remains ever near.[6]

Thirdly, world citizens face the challenge of crime and violence. These criminal activities range from individual crime to organised crime, including terrorism. Rapid population growth and the overcrowding of cities provide a fertile environment for both types of crime. To again make an example of the city of Cape Town - although one of South Africa's prime tourist attractions, it is also the murder capital of the country and has been rated the 11th most violent city in the world. The presence of crime, therefore, is not only limited to so-called informal settlements and townships, but presents a challenge to all cities of the world as well as all their citizens.

Fourthly, we have the enormous impact of technological advancement in the areas of information, communication and so-called artificial intelligence. Often described as the most disruptive force in the advancement of the human race, the so-called Fourth Industrial Revolution has enriched our lives in many ways and has led to breakthroughs that would have been unthinkable a decade or three ago. The challenge facing humanity is finding ways on how technological advancement can benefit all of us and not only some of us.

Fifthly, is the integration of ethical conduct into everything we do. How governments, business and civil society do business always has an impact on all of us, particularly on the poorest of the poor. Very often, those who flock to the cities of the world in search of a better life for themselves and their offspring are left forgotten on the fringes of otherwise thriving and affluent cities. In many instances, this does not happen because there is a lack of resources, but simply because nobody really cares.

6

Finally yet importantly (on my summarised list) is the challenge of what is often referred to as the challenge of being inclusive. When matters of global significance affect global citizens, it always helps a great deal when genuine consideration is given to the meaningful involvement of those who, consciously or unconsciously, may be excluded, including but not limited to the poor, women, the aged, youth, children and the disabled. Very often, these individuals and groups are treated as the targets and recipients of the benevolence of gracious decision makers. As the warning always comes to those who claim they are solving all the world's problems - 'nothing about us without us'.

However, this new global challenge named COVID-19, would, in a short time, overshadow all the other problems of the world and take centre stage.

Chapter 2
THE START OF THE TROUBLE

'I have told you these things, so that in me you may have peace.
In this world you will have trouble. But take heart!
I have overcome the world.'
John 16:33 (New International Version)

It started during December 2019. So they say.

There are those who suggest that the trouble might have started much earlier. First, they say, was a 43-year-old fish market worker in France[7] who suffered very serious chest pains way back in November 2019. He was diagnosed with a lung infection. Two different tests conducted on old samples revealed that the patient, in fact, recovered from a new, highly infectious strain of flu virus. Similar reports were emanating from Sweden[8] where it was also found that someone was infected with the new virus. Probably, as was the case in France, as far back as November 2019. A spokesperson for the World Health Organisation said this was not surprising and that it was possible that more early cases may be found.

Nevertheless, apparently something went wrong in the city of Wuhan, in the province of Hubei in China - a sprawling metropolis that about eleven million people call home. Whatever it was and whatever the origin, the impact on the world as we know it would be devastating, to say the least. Millions would become infected with a virus, now notoriously known as the coronavirus, causing a life threatening disease baptised COVID-19. While many infected persons would recover, at the time of writing, more than 370 000 of the world's citizens would pay with their lives.

8

The internet is awash with coverage about the impact of the COVID-19 disease. Many of these reports are from reliable, well-known sources, but there are also others, who find time to spread controversial conspiracy theories and still others who openly distribute what has become known as fake news. One may find information online about good diets to follow, natural remedies as well as tips on how to conduct oneself responsibly or irresponsibly during the pandemic, but according to the more reliable sources, the story goes more or less like this.

A sudden outbreak of what was initially thought to be pneumonia occurred in the city of Wuhan during December 2019. All of a sudden, an increasing number of people in the city of Wuhan, complaining about symptoms ranging from fever, weakness, difficulty breathing and loss of appetite, were seeking medical assistance. It was not long before suspicions grew that what doctors and other medical personnel were dealing with was the appearance of a new mutation of a virus known as corona, so called because, under a microscope, the protein attachments to the virus make it look like a crown.

Enter the scientists.[9] On 11 and 12 February 2020 about 400 scientists from around the world gathered to discuss a response to the coronavirus causing the new outbreak. Some gathered physically and others joined online. On the same day (11 February 2020), the director general of the World Health Organisation made a statement during which he revealed some disturbing statistics to the world. Already more than 1 000 people of more than 42 000 who were infected had already died in China,[10] with most of the deaths having occurred in Wuhan, Hubei province. He also made known that the virus had already traveled outside of China with one death out of 393 confirmed cases in 24 countries.

As far as the new outbreak of the coronavirus was concerned, amongst scientists there seemed to be agreement about the following. The virus had its origin with an animal, probably a bat, and later found a human host. In Wuhan, where the outbreak started, most of those infected visited or worked at a market where live animals were kept, slaughtered and sold. There seemed to be a high mortality rate amongst those over the age of 70. Even those in their sixties were advised to proceed with caution. The symptoms might include high fever, weakness and shortness of breath. Some might even host the virus without displaying any of the symptoms, particularly smaller children.

It was told that the steps taken by the Chinese authorities might have limited the impact, cost and damage of the virus significantly. At the time of writing, more than three months after Wuhan went into lockdown, the city was slowly returning to some form of normal. More than 4 800 deaths out of about 83 000 infections were recorded. Of these, about 80 000 had recovered from the disease. Amongst the many measures introduced, China implemented what might be described as the most severe travel restrictions ever introduced before in its history. While China would have no shortage of critique regarding the way it communicated with the world during the very early days of the outbreak, there would be many countries and cities who would have to take a leaf from their book on how to deal with the crisis.

While things were returning to "normal" in China, the virus travelled abroad, and with devastating consequences.

Chapter 3
THE CORONAVIRUS GOES ABROAD

'If the owner of a house knew the time when the thief would come,
you can be sure that he would stay awake and not let
the thief break into his house.'
Matthew 24:43 (Good News Translation)

It is believed that the coronavirus arrived in Italy[11] on 31 January 2020.

Apparently, two Chinese tourists in the city of Rome tested positive for the virus. About a week later, an Italian man who returned from Wuhan, China was confirmed as the third case in Italy. As would later be the trend in most parts of the world, the number of confirmed cases in Italy started growing rapidly and by the beginning of March, the virus had spread to most parts of Italy. As at 6 May 2020, Italy had more than 214 000 confirmed cases with more than 90 000 of those being described as active cases. At the time of writing, out of about 214 000 confirmed cases about 30 000 Italians had already died from the coronavirus. More than 93 000 had already recovered.

Less than 1 000 miles away, in Spain,[12] the virus made its first appearance, as was the case in Italy, on 31 January 2020. By mid-March, cases were confirmed in all 50 provinces. The country declared a state of alarm on 14 March 2020 and went into lockdown for two weeks. At the end of March, most of the confirmed cases, as well as deaths in Spain were recorded in Madrid. By this time, the Spanish death toll was higher than it was recorded in China, where the virus originated. At the time of writing, Spain had more than 256 000 confirmed cases with more than 26 000 deaths and more than

163 000 recoveries. The only country with a higher death toll than that of Spain was the United States of America (USA).

The coronavirus made its first appearance in the USA[13] in the state of New York. It is understood that on 1 March 2020, a healthcare worker from Manhattan returned from Iran on 25 February 2020, but displayed no symptoms immediately after her arrival in the United States. The second confirmed case in the USA was on 3 March 2020. He was a lawyer who lived in New Rochelle, Westchester County, north of New York City. At the time of writing, there were more than 1.2 million confirmed cases in the USA and more than 74 000 had died from the coronavirus. More than 170 000 infected persons had already recovered from the virus in the United States of America.

The first confirmed case of the coronavirus in my home country, South Africa,[14] was on 5 March 2020. The first patient to be confirmed positive with the virus arrived in the province of KwaZulu-Natal with a tour party, which included his wife and eight other people, from Italy. On 15 March 2020, our President Cyril Ramaphosa announced measures on how to combat the Covid 19 pandemic and just eight days later, on 23 March 2020, declared a 21-day nationwide lockdown. New regulations were published to enforce the strict measures that were introduced. The lockdown period was later extended by a further 14 days. At the time of writing South Africa had recorded more than 50 000 confirmed cases with more than 1000 deaths and more than 30 000 recoveries.

News of South Africa's first confirmed cases spread like wildfire and there was a sense of alarm all over the nation, having, through the press and other news media, been made aware of the devastation that had already been caused in countries like China and Italy. Almost immediately, there was a flurry of panic buying and certain items like toilet rolls, hand sanitiser and masks suddenly flew off supermarket shelves, followed by exorbitant increases in the prices of those items. By mid-March, the South African newspaper headlines were speculating about a looming lockdown and the announcement of crisis plans by cabinet. The measures to be introduced would include, inter alia, a travel ban, airport closures and strict limitations on public gatherings. Initially, during the period from 15 to 26 March 2020, public meetings were allowed to continue, albeit with some restrictions.[15]

Public gatherings were limited to a maximum of 100[16] in attendance subject to the rules of social distancing and sanitising of the hands and avoiding contact with one's face. Over the weekend from 19 to 22 March 2020, the larger churches were compelled to have multiple services and others already used to having multiple services, had to increase the number of services significantly. Already over that weekend, churches felt the impact on both their attendance figures and income. Then, on 23 March 2020,[17] the president made his second announcement within an eight-day period. A 21-day lockdown would be enforced which would include a total ban on public gatherings including, amongst other, sports events, concerts and religious gatherings of any kind and any number of people. Some of the newspaper headlines made it quite clear what we were in for - total lockdown, standstill, stay inside, it is a national disaster, the headlines exclaimed.

Chapter 4
THE DAY THEY LOCKED THE CHURCH DOORS

'For you shut the door of the Kingdom of Heaven in people's faces.
You won't go in yourselves, and you don't let others enter either.'
Matthew 23:13b (New Living Translation)

Not only was the Church told to leave the building, but also to stay out of the building.

In all fairness, initially, so was almost everybody else. In South Africa, as was the case in the rest of the world, and in most countries, only those organisations providing an essential service were allowed to continue doing business under the first stage of lockdown known as Level 5. These would include, but not be limited to places like hospitals, pharmacies, supermarkets and essential services provided by the state such as the army, correctional facilities and all law enforcement agencies. All public gatherings including sports events, concerts and festivals, as well as day-to-day activities like walking the dog or going out for a walk or a jog would be declared unlawful. This would be in force for 21 days from midnight on 26 March 2020 and later be extended by another 14 days until 30 April 2020.[18]

Then, after more than 35 days on the so-called Level 5 of lockdown, the lockdown period in South Africa was extended indefinitely, with some relaxation of the lockdown rules. This new level of lockdown was referred to as Level 4.[19] The nation was advised, that, as time goes on, there would be a gradual opening up of the economy going down through Levels 3 and 2 to Level 1. As in the rest of the world, life in South Africa then changed dramatically and the economy was dealt a threatening blow by the extended period of lockdown. The lockdown fatigue and devastation caused by the rules and regulations was

14

giving birth to a new restlessness that was threatening to turn into lawlessness.

The state president of South Africa was in an invidious position. How to find the balance between the priorities of the nation's health and the health of the economy? Right from his first announcement on 15 March 2020, the choices were going to be hard and not always popular. During the initial 21-day period of lockdown the leaders of all political parties, business leaders, religious leaders and the whole nation, so it seemed, rallied around the president. Even the most vocal critics of the president seemed to have retired into silence, but by the end of May, in a column written for a Sunday paper a former opposition party leader would declare (very disrespectfully) that the president had gone 'from a secular saint to a "mampara"'.[20]

Everyone seemed to understand that we were in a war situation and as the 29 March 2020 headline of a Sunday newspaper put it, 'It was a war we had to win[21]' and as yet another headline of one of the Cape Town dailies rallied the day after the president's first announcement, 'We are in this together'. At that early stage, it seemed as though all South Africans were all in it together. Perhaps the one benefit of our young democracy that we should be grateful for is the freedom of the media to report, without fear or favour, on what was happening on the ground - on a daily, even hourly basis.

The first 21-day lockdown period would last from midnight on 26 March 2020 to 16 April 2020. Then it was extended by another 14 days until 30 April 2020. However, it would not be long after the announcement of the extension of those additional two weeks, that things would begin to unravel. The very same Sunday newspaper that initially inspired the nation to 'win the war' now declared on its front page headline of 19 April 2020, 'Hunger stalks South Africa[22]'. In fact,

15

before the first three weeks of lockdown ended, the daily newspapers in my city, Cape Town, were already placing headlines on their front pages that read, 'We are hungry' and 'Hungry and angry'.

Perhaps one day, when the history of this time is written, the most mismanaged project of the lockdown period will be the one that was supposed to bring urgent alleviation to the most vulnerable households in the nation, or as they are sometimes described, the poorest of the poor - the distribution of food parcels or food vouchers to these households. The press kept the nation informed of the corruption and mismanagement of the project that was supposed to get much needed food to the hungry and destitute.

'Food parcel looting hits the poor[23]' and 'Unrest over food parcels[24]' shouted the headlines within days of the food parcels becoming available.

Chapter 5
LIFE UNDER LOCKDOWN

'Come, my people, enter your chambers,
And shut your doors behind you;
Hide yourself, as it were, for a little moment,
until the indignation is past.'
Isaiah 26:20 (New King James Version)

Then came the president's next announcement[25] - the lockdown period would continue indefinitely after 30 April 2020, albeit with some relaxation of the lockdown rules. By this time not only had the number of confirmed and active cases of COVID-19 in the country increased, but the number of deaths also seemed to indicate a worrisome trajectory. The extended and indefinite period would be described as Level 4. It would be the start of the gradual opening up of the economy through Levels 3, 2 and eventually Level 1. At the time of writing, it was not clear how long each level would last and what exactly would occur during Levels 3 and 2. By now, the nation was on an ever-increasing scale, beginning to display signs of a growing lockdown fatigue.

During a press briefing (these press briefings were taking place quite regularly), one of the cabinet ministers reminded the nation that the decisions that were being taken, as well as the regulations that were being enforced was based on science and not common sense.[26] However, up to that time no explanation had been offered on two decisions that were backtracked on. First, there was the science-based decision to allow only three people per minibus taxi, only to be changed to minibus taxis being allowed to be filled to 70% capacity.[27] The other example was the scientific decision with regard to the relaxation of regulations, as it would apply to the selling of tobacco

17

and cigarette products.[28] A rather unsatisfactory explanation was offered for the sudden change of heart when the decision makers backtracked on that one.

In the meantime, the wheels of the South African economy was grinding slower and slower with more and more voices beginning to call for greater relaxation of the lockdown rules or for a complete end to the lockdown. More and more households were joining the ranks of those who found themselves without food to eat and many small business owners were indicating that they might not be able to continue with business after lockdown. Even bigger companies were either applying for business rescue or liquidation. The health of the nation versus the resuscitation of the economy - what was it going to be? There was no sign of the country's leader. For about two weeks, the president just simply disappeared off the radar.

There seemed to appear fine cracks within the ranks of government. There were those observers who saw the announcement by one of the cabinet ministers to withdraw the earlier commitment by the country's president to allow the sale of tobacco and cigarette products as an undermining action.[29] The president himself would later defend the backtracking as a collective decision based on new information.[30] The finance minister[31] would publicly disagree with decisions taken by the so-called command council and a former finance minister[32] would describe some of the decisions of the command council as irrational. It seemed that after almost 50 days under lockdown, the patience, not only of the nation, but also some individuals inside the decision making structures was wearing thin.

When the president re-emerged on Wednesday, 13 May 2020,[33] to address the South African nation there was high expectation in the air that he would be announcing some form of relief in terms of the further relaxation of restrictions. Great was the disappointment when he skirted the issues in his eight-page speech, adding very little or no new information to what was said before and already known to the people of South Africa. Up to this point, two things that were becoming a trademark of these announcements by the president was his familiar introduction of '... my fellow South Africans...' and his complete silence about the religious sector or the Church for that matter. As silent as the president was, so it seemed, were the national Church leaders in the country.

The restrictions on public gatherings, of course, were not imposed only on the religious sector or the Church, but on all gatherings of every kind where crowds would have difficulty maintaining the hygiene and social distancing rules. These would include, but not be limited to sports gatherings, horse races, concerts, watching movies in theatres, hanging out at the mall. The world was dealing with a highly infectious virus that seemed to thrive on the social interaction between humans. However, the government was offering all kinds of financial assistance to individuals and businesses, including assistance to the entertainment industry where moviemakers and actors amongst others, was finding it hard to make ends meet. The Church, the clergy, their families and their flocks, it seemed, were not very high on the agenda of those politicians and church leaders who were perhaps not feeling the pinch of not receiving their salaries at the end of the month.

Chapter 6
NO MORE PUBLIC GATHERINGS – THE EFFECT
ON THE CHURCH

'Remember Him before the door to life's opportunities
is closed and the sound of work fades...'
Ecclesiastes 12:4a (New Living Translation)

In the beginning of the lockdown period, the restrictions on public
gatherings was embraced by church leaders with appreciation and
understanding. It was not going to be an easy call. Churches work
with crowds. In many instances with crowds that number thousands of
people. Understandably then, religious organisations were regarded
as public gatherings, where the challenge of safe hygiene and
effective social distancing would be a daunting task. All over the world,
with very few exceptions, so it seemed, for the purposes of lockdown,
the Church would not be regarded as an essential service to the
nations. Here in South Africa, it is not impossible that, perhaps, things
were made worse for the Church because of significant noncompliance by unwise church leaders over the weekend of 19 to 22
March 2020, when there was a limit imposed of not more than 100
people per gathering.[34]

In addition, the few independent church leaders who, right from the
start, protested against the complete closure of church services were
repeatedly reminded of what happened at a specific church event that
took place from 9 to 11 March 2020 in a place called Ribblesdale,
Bloemfontein.[35] The occasion was called the Jerusalem Prayer
Breakfast, hosted by an organisation called the Divine Restoration
Ministries. Apparently, a well-known South African preacher, as well as
politicians from one of the smaller opposition parties attended this

20

event. It was understood that five overseas guests amongst the 895 who attended the event had been tested positive for COVID-19.

However, long before the arrival of the deadly coronavirus and its relative COVID-19 in South Africa, there was already a battle taking place between the Church and an organ of the South African state, namely the Commission for the Promotion and Protection of the Rights of Cultural, Religious and Linguistic Communities, the CRL Rights Commission (CRL),[36] for short. This is an independent chapter nine institution in South Africa that derives its mandate from the South African Constitution by way of the Commission for the Promotion and Protection of the Rights of Cultural, Religious and Linguistic Communities Act of 2002.

The so-called CRL is mandated to promote respect for and further the protection of the rights of cultural, religious and linguistic communities; promote and develop peace, friendship, humanity, tolerance, national unity among and within cultural, religious and linguistic communities on the basis of equality, non-discrimination and free association; to promote the right of communities to develop their historically diminished heritage and to recognise community councils. To cut a long story short, the establishment of this commission is widely regarded by the broader Church in South Africa as an attempt of government to exercise greater control over the Church.

The Church was and is still very vocal against this commission, but as far as the restrictive lockdown rules and regulations were concerned, it seemed as if the Church had taken a vow of silence. Perhaps the words of the wise old Solomon should not be forgotten during these challenging times, 'If you are weak in a crisis, then you are weak indeed.[37]' The Church, it seems, is hopeful, that after bowing to government during the long period of lockdown, she might take up her fight and continue against the so-called CRL as a strong Church. God forbid that the Church wakes up to find, like Sampson, her hair was cut during her lockdown sleep with the sharp scissors of her own silence.

Time will tell whether it was the right thing to do on the part of church leaders to exercise their right to remain silent during a time when many of their own was going through the most traumatising and devastating period of their lives and careers. Thousands (if not tens of thousands) of homes of clergy went without food and electricity and other essential items while being instructed to still continue to care for the flock (from a distance) by leaders who, in all probability and respectfully, were receiving their full salaries on time at the end of every month.

As the apostle Paul cautioned, 'If anyone does not provide for his own, and especially his own household, he has denied the faith and is worse than an unbeliever.[38]'

Chapter 7
THE SILENCE OF THE CHURCH

'Justice is turned back, And righteousness stands afar off;
For truth is fallen in the street, And equity cannot enter.'
Isaiah 59:14 (New King James Version)

'Qui tacet consentire videtur, ubi loqui debuit ac potuit'

The above Latin expression, loosely translated means, 'He who is silent, when he ought to have spoken and was able to, is taken to agree.' It is the humble opinion of this author that the Church has a voice, has always had a voice and will always have a voice. It is further this author's view that this voice does not have be wasted in any frivolous conversation, but when the moment demands it, this voice should always be heard. On 12 April 2020, an influential voice of the South African Church was heard in an article published in a Sunday newspaper, under the heading, 'Virus unites all of God's children[39]'. The writer of the article goes on to make some potent observations with regard to the present situation and makes some thought provoking comments about the future.

In the fourth paragraph the writer warns the readers that no one is immune and that the virus will spread fast and far if we allow it to and will cause havoc. In the fifth paragraph the readers are further encouraged to pay close attention to the medical expertise and give our full support to government's priority. The aspects of bravery, foresight, strength, courage and the fact that the believers do not have a spirit of fear are well highlighted in the seventh paragraph and closing words of the article. In the article the writer goes on to remind the political class that we need to promote the moral and ethical handling of our resources both during the crisis and into the future and quotes the president of the republic of South Africa when he called for 'a new moral economy that has people and their welfare at its centre'.

By any standard, an excellent article that touches on the real issues that really matter. Nevertheless, I would risk making a respectful enquiry - did we (the Church) do enough when we ought to have spoken? On the other hand, was there no situation before or after 12 April 2020 that demanded that the voice of the Church be heard? Was it safe to change from three people per minibus taxi to a 70% filled taxi? Was it safe before reversing the decision and was it safe after? Does the virus not have an opportunity to travel fast and far in a 70% filled taxi? Moreover, if a 70% filled taxi is safe, what is so unsafe about a 50% filled church building, where a record can be kept of those in attendance and strict application of hygiene rules and social distancing can be enforced and monitored? What about the president's about turn regarding the decision about the sale of cigarettes and tobacco products? In addition, the looting of food for the poor? Was that something to remain silent about or was it awkward for the Church to get involved because it was about the deadly habit of smoking?

There was the crisis of the reopening of schools. Another project that was not managed so elegantly, albeit under extremely difficult conditions. Again, time will tell whether the idea of Professor Jonathan Jansen to scrap the entire 2020 school year[40] was so farfetched. Briefly, Jansen suggested that, when schools reopen, they should continue as normal in terms of teaching of the curriculum without putting pressure on teachers. Every learner from Grade 1 to Grade 11 should be passed at the end of the year and the year 2021 must be used to reorganise the curriculum. The Grade 12 learners who hope to go to university, should be accepted based on their preliminary acceptance results from Grade 11. The good professor further suggested that universities and schools must sit together to plan a bridging curriculum for these progressed Grade 12 learners. 'It would be unfair to ask teachers to try and make up for lost time', the professor warned.

If there is an inkling of truth in the Latin expression, then those who remain silent loudly declare their agreement. In their own defence, they might declare that there was nothing that could be done. In particular, when history is written and it is found that there was so-called consultation with national leaders of the Church. Will history judge the South African Church that the taxi industry had more persuasive negotiators than the Church? Or will the Church in perpetuity claim that the concern for the health and wellbeing of the faithful and other citizens was the biggest consideration of the Church. If the health and wellbeing of the citizens was of such a concern, how safe were the faithful travelling in those minibuses. Will we ever know if perhaps thousands of infections took root while commuters travelled in 70% filled minibuses that were criss-crossing the country?

While it may be conceded that His Excellency, President Ramaphosa, at the outset, was presented with an arduous task of choosing a balance between the health of the nation and the economy, this author is not so sure whether, from that point onwards, the president and his so-called National Command Council on COVID-19 had been consistent in all respects. Time will tell whether science, common sense or political infighting prevailed. Perhaps one day the nation will know what happened behind the scenes before the instances of backtracking on decisions and promises. History will also be the judge of whether the voice of the Church was heard when it was supposed to be heard or whether, when placed in the scales of history, the Church of our Lord Jesus Christ, (our leader who himself was crucified as an enemy of the state), respectfully, might be found wanting. Or was the silence of the South African Church perhaps to do with the fact that she has strong ties to government,[41] as a Sunday paper suggested on Pentecost Sunday?

Chapter 8
THE SILENCE OF MY OWN DENOMINATION

'An open rebuke is better than hidden love.'
Proverbs 27:5 (New Living Translation)

My own background is what may be called Classic Pentecostal. The denomination where I live out my vocation as a pastor is one of the largest in South Africa and it has a footprint in Africa and in many parts of the world. Before the arrival of the coronavirus and COVID-19, the broader Church, across the globe, was experiencing a renewed phase of growth and a significant part of that growth was in Africa. The Pentecostal movement was at the forefront of this new surge within the community of believers. As one observer remarked, 'the Church was back in business'. Within my denomination, I am responsible for the leadership of a multi-site church in the city of Cape Town and I have oversight responsibility (regional chairperson) over another 50 churches in the city.

A collective of four national office bearers, namely a president, deputy president, general secretary and general treasurer, leads the denomination on a day-to-day basis. Three times per year, the four national office bearers, joined by the chairpersons of 43 regions across the country and the national leaders of departments meet as the National Leadership Forum, the national decision making body of the denomination. The day after the country's president made his first announcement on 15 March 2020, we started our four-day meeting in the city of Cape Town. After this meeting, we issued a statement wherein we implored all our members across the country to comply fully with the restrictions as laid down in the state president's speech of 15 March 2020.

27

As things unfolded over the next week, it became necessary for the country's president to make his second speech on 23 March 2020 during which he declared a national state of disaster. This national state of disaster would be accompanied by even stricter restrictions, particularly on public gatherings, which was what Church life was all about - the fellowship of the saints, as the Scripture says. Again, a further statement was issued by our denomination, wherein the faithful were earnestly encouraged to give their full support and compliance to the rules laid down in the regulations. Members were told to stay at home, except for essential reasons and pastors were advised to offer prayers and pastoral support over the phone, if possible, but always at a distance.

This clear instruction to the leaders and members of the denomination was, of course, the right thing to do. However, it was not long before the realities of life under lockdown started kicking in. Within the poorer parts of the denomination, local leaders were discovering that people were not really giving the 'Lord's Tithe' through the online banking channels available to them. Cash was king in the township, so it seemed. Local church income dropped by as much as two thirds of what it was before lockdown. This led to a situation where the pastor's salary and other expenses could not be fully paid and, in some instances, not paid at all. Our regional office (in other church traditions a region would be similar to a diocese) received calls for help from more than 20 out of 50 churches in distress.

It makes sense, if there is little or no income in the pastor's household, things would be the same or worse in the homes of most of the members. Still, under these conditions spiritual leaders had to be available for the flock, to comfort, support and strengthen them during a time of worldwide crisis. It was painful listening to their very reasonable protestations during their time of untold suffering. How can people be safe in a taxi, but not in church? It made no sense to them. How can they be safe in queues where no social distance is adhered to, but not in church? Meanwhile, things were deteriorating as the coronavirus continued its path of death and destruction.

The infection rate, as well as the number of deaths in the country was steadily climbing. The initial lockdown period of 21 days had already been extended by a further 14 days. It would continue indefinitely on what would be called Level 4, where the initial restrictions (Level 5) would be somewhat relaxed and some industries allowed to reopen and employers and employees allowed to return to work. Already it became quite clear that the church would be last in line. The voices of discontent amongst local church leaders could be heard through the social networks and other media. Alongside this frustration of local church leaders, a lot of resentment was brewing because others, it seemed, were allowed to flout lockdown rules with complete impunity. Therefore, this author wrote his first email to the national office bearers of his denomination on 14 April 2020.

Chapter 9
DID THE AFM OF SA BREAK HER SILENCE?

'The rich rule over the poor, and the borrower is slave to the lender.'
Proverbs 22:7 (New International Version)

Perhaps, now, I should use the opportunity to interrupt myself and make a few things clear to the reader. I am a loyal and disciplined member of my denomination and I have only the deepest respect for my leaders and all my colleagues. Any differences of opinion contained in these pages are shared in the context of speaking my mind in love. The views expressed are my own observations of situations and decisions and not a judgement of any kind. The very reason I chose to communicate with my own leaders was precisely due to my respect for them, instead of venting my views on social networks and in the media, as many other church leaders were doing at the time.

Within a matter of hours, I received my president's kind response to my email of 14 April 2020, even though I indicated in my correspondence that no response to my email was required. I did that because for a number reasons, amongst other I wanted bring to my leaders' attention my concern that the voice of our denomination was silent when, in my humble opinion, the situation was demanding that we speak. Secondly, I realised that it might not be my last correspondence on the subject and I did not want to burden them with repeatedly having to decide on a collective response to my email. I also shared with them my concern for the wellness of the denomination's pastors and their families, as well as vital and useful information that could be placed at the disposal of our pastors, leaders and members that was not forthcoming.

After expressing my view that perhaps the Church in South Africa (of which our denomination was a part) was not engaging robustly enough with our government, I conveyed to them as humbly and as concisely as I could, what I meant by the silence of the Church. I raised the question whether we were not perhaps being compliant with the lockdown regulations without fully applying our minds to what we were being told as opposed to what was being done in front of our very own eyes. I shared with them what was, by now, my favourite example of how one could be safe in a minibus taxi filled to 70% capacity and not in a 70% filled church building where an attendance record of members could be kept and where people who attended could be traced. I questioned how taxi commuters who changed taxis all the time could be traced.

I went as far as making known my humble view that when all of this was over, a very real possibility existed that history might not judge the Church and her leaders very kindly. I was almost begging that we should be paying closer attention to the suffering in pastoral households and other households. I shared with them my burden that one day when the history of this time came to be written, the blame for being silent might be laid squarely at the doors of us, as church leaders who were too weak to confront our government about the risks of exposing the nation by allowing 70% filled minibus taxis on our roads. And if we, as church leaders, continued to agree (through our silence) that there were no risks involved in a 70% filled minibus taxi, then, we were also agreeing with our government that a church building filled to 70% capacity, where a record of attendees could be kept within a controlled environment, was much more dangerous than a 70% filled taxi.

My second email was sent to my leaders on 23 April 2020, two days after the president of South Africa made his second announcement within a timespan of eight days. It was about the R500 billion[42] (mostly borrowed money) and how it was going to be distributed to the nation as relief for businesses and individuals. The amounts from the largest to the smallest were R200 billion, R100 billion, R80 billion, R50 billion, R40 billion, R20 billion, R20 billion and R2 billion. The distribution would ostensibly be as follows. Amongst other, the largest part would be a R200 billion loan guarantee for businesses to pay salaries and suppliers. A further R100 billion would be allocated to protect and create jobs. The Reserve Bank would unlock at least R80 billion to provide liquidity to the financial system. Another R50 billion would be made available as social relief for the most vulnerable families and R40 billion would be used for income support payments for workers.

Municipalities would be allocated R20 billion and another R20 billion was set aside for hunger relief and distress". Again, it seemed, the poor were last, but not least. The smallest allocation of only R2 billion would be used to assist small, medium and micro enterprises. If officials could not be found faithful in the handling of mere food parcels,[43] who was going to be in charge of making sure that critically required relief of this magnitude reached deserving recipients? This, it seemed, was none of the Church's business. Even if, behind the scenes, away from the public's eyes and ears, indeed there was quiet engagement going on with those in power - can private correspondence be regarded as the breaking of one's silence on a public matter?

Chapter 10
THE SILENCE OF CITY MOVEMENTS

'Wisdom is the principal thing; Therefore get wisdom.
And in all your getting, get understanding.'
Proverbs 4:7 (New King James Version)

Over the last number of years there has been, in cities all across the world, the rise of what may be referred to as city gospel movements. What is a city gospel movement? I actually found a response to this question on the internet. According to that definition, 'a city gospel movement is a united, holistic, sustainable effort by the citywide Church to seek the peace and prosperity of their city'. Further clarity as to the meaning of the words united, holistic and sustainable were also provided along with the definition. United, 'the united Church in a city working together with other sectors of society'. Holistic, 'living out and proclaiming the gospel in word and deed'. Sustainable, 'long-term vision and commitment to the city'. This type of movement also exists in my own city.

It is this author's view that, in the city of Cape Town, there are a great many individuals and organisations making a very positive difference in and to our city. There are prayer movements, evangelistic movements, ecumenical movements and many other organisations doing ministry among the destitute, the broken, the hurt, the vulnerable, even the addicted and the outcasts of society. There are definite limitations to what these bodies can achieve when each of these function on their own. The city and its citizens derive the maximum benefit when there are collaborative efforts, and respect and appreciation amongst each other for the contribution of all who want to make a difference in their city.

33

As a city lover myself, it would, therefore, become inevitable that, in my own city, I would become involved in one or more of these city movements. One of these is an influential ecumenical body where most of the larger denominations are represented, as well as para-church organisations and representatives from independent churches. The organisation's reason for existence is explained more or less as follows in their constitution. It exists for the promotion of dialogue and action, initiated primarily from within the Christian community, including church and para-church structures, with the purpose of playing a meaningful role with regard to the identification and implementation of practical transformational initiatives in consultation with relevant stakeholders, in the context of reconciliation, restoration and restitution.[44]

Right from the beginning of the lockdown period, this ecumenical body saw the need for involvement in the situation that was playing itself out all over our city. There was the immediate and urgent issue of thousands of households in the grip of hunger with government's promised food parcels taking the longest time to reach those devastated families. The urgency of the situation led to hastily made plans and frantic attempts at finding willing donors and willing helping hands. It was heartwarming to see the Church in action. One of the larger denominations made a significant financial contribution while others offered resources in kind. The need was huge and the task was daunting. We were not going to reach everybody, but when the crisis presented itself, the Church went on the move.

Then there was the matter of the relocation of the city's homeless people. The mayor and other city officials will probably admit that this very difficult endeavour could have been managed in a more, how shall I say, elegant manner. The level of transparency in communication with all the relevant stakeholders was particularly poor.

A visit to one particular site by Doctors Without Borders ended in the city receiving a very negative report about conditions in the tented camp where the homeless were being accommodated, as well as a lot of bad press. City movements need unity to be effective value-adding instruments in their cities so they always have to guard that one problem in the city does not jeopardise future cooperation by all stakeholders. The situation in the so-called Strandfontein Camp was one such situation.

Once again, this author became frustrated at the lack of attention and response being given to some of government's decisions in this organisation as well. I tried as best as I could to see if, within our ranks, someone could explain to me the complete silence with regard to the roundabout turn the government was making after announcing decisions to the nation, in particular the decision to significantly increase the passengers per taxi after announcing that only three passengers would be allowed in a minibus. I was reminded that we were a regional movement and although I had to concede that we were indeed a regional city movement, I was of the view that most of the denominations represented had national mouthpieces and there was also the South African Council of Churches where most of our denominations were members. Surely, we could lobby them to break the silence of the Church? However, it seemed to me that my words were falling on deaf ears. It was only later that I became aware that there was division within our own ranks about the re-opening of churches.

Chapter 11
THE LEADER OF THE CHURCH

'...I will build my church, and the gates of hell
shall not prevail against it.'
Matthew 16:18b (English Standard Version)

I have been a pastor for longer than 30 years. I was trained, like thousands of others before and after me, to preach the good news from the pulpit. Over time, you become one with your vocation and the rhythms of your duties, as well as the accompanying rituals. However, all of this is done from the security and safety of the sanctuary. Some preparation and effort is required before the believers gather on Sunday. Not only the preparation of a message or sermon, but also preparation by the essential ministry teams, including the worship team, musicians, choir, ushers and parking attendants. All of this culminates in the weekly gathering on Sunday - in the building.

Then, to be told to leave the building and stay at home was not the kind of news that fell nicely on the believers' ears. Truth be told, about two thousand years ago, the instruction from the leader of the movement was exactly that - to leave the building. In my humble opinion, that is really what the Church has been all along - a movement - an organisation on the go. The leader of the movement called Christianity can be traced back to a crucifixion on a wooden cross early in the first century during the Roman era. Jesus of Nazareth, as he was known, was executed by being impaled on a cross. A death, we are told, reserved for criminals, more particularly, for those regarded as enemies of the state.

During his relatively short lifespan, Jesus crisscrossed first century Palestine, mostly by foot, accompanied by a core group of twelve

36

disciples. According to the scriptures, at times, this number of disciples increased to about 70 or 72. A summary of his brief lifespan on earth (roughly 33 years) is captured within the pages of the four Gospels in the New Testament of the Bible. From these reports, we learn of a man who had compassion for those who lived on the fringes of society, the downtrodden, the marginalised, and the outcasts of the human race. We understand that he was described as a wine bibber and a glutton, a friend of sinners. His short earthly life was marked by conflict with organised religion, to the point that he turned the tables of the moneychangers within the temple precinct.

He preached a message of love, forgiveness and social concern, and on one occasion, when the instruction seemed a certain impossibility, encouraged his disciples with the words, 'you give them something to eat'. It could be argued that he demonstrated a disregard for the social conventions of his day, by mixing and mingling with all kinds of people, even those who were not of his own ethnic group. He seemed to go out of his way to touch those cast out by society as unclean, unwanted and unwelcome. He visited neighbourhoods regarded as no go areas during his day.

In the Gospels, on a number of occasions, he predicted that those in authority[45] would execute him. However, he also made it quite clear that he was laying his own life down and that no one was going to take his life away from him.[46] He went as far as predicting that he would overcome death and rise again. After his resurrection from death, the risen Jesus met with his disciples and gave an instruction, which could be interpreted to be the establishment of an alternative empire (kingdom) here on earth. As our Lord Jesus himself put it, 'I will build My church, and the gates of Hell shall not prevail against it.[47]'

These famous words once uttered by our Lord Jesus Christ, through the ages, have given hope and inspiration to countless church leaders to continue with their efforts, even against the greatest odds under very challenging conditions. There are also those who argue that this quote is an anachronism that was put into the mouth of Jesus by Bible writers. That is an argument for another day. A well-known US church leader has, in fact, gone much further than our Lord Jesus Christ by declaring that the local church is the hope of the world and that the positive impact of the work done by church leaders far outweighs the impact of the contributions made by leaders in other spheres, including business and political leaders.[48]

The same church leader goes on to argue that unlike leaders in business, government and the education sector, church leaders actually have the power to change the world. He continues along these lines and asserts that church leaders have the potential to be the most influential force on planet earth. If we accept and believe the words of Jesus that 'the gates of hell will not prevail against the church' and if we buy into the idea that the Church is the most influential force on planet earth, should the Church not be in some sort of acceleration mode? Or at least speak up a little louder?

Chapter 12
BUT WHO IS THE 'CHURCH'?

'You are the light of the world - like a city
on a hilltop that cannot be hidden.'
Matthew 5:14 (New Living Translation)

For the longest time now there has been this phenomenon called the Church.

Now is perhaps a good time to remind the reader that whenever the word Church appears in this book with a capital letter "C" it refers either to the worldwide movement generally referred to as 'Christians' or the broader Church (Christians) in my home country, South Africa. Then, on the other hand, when the small letter 'c' is used it might refer to the local church where I am pastor or any other local church anywhere in the world. Whenever it is used in the latter context, it refers to that group of individuals who gather regularly (mostly on Sundays) to give expression to their spiritual beliefs through, amongst other, prayer, worship and listening to the Word of God. These regular meetings may take place in facilities ranging from large cathedrals and stadiums to temporary shacks, even under trees - with many other types of venues in-between.

This group of people who gather (mostly on Sundays) have often been accused (fairly or unfairly) of being inward looking, that is, focused on and, with some exceptions, concerned only about those within their own circle - those who believe like them, sound like them, look like them and dress like them. While there may be some evidence of concern and care about the situation in the external environment outside the church walls, largely it may appear to the outsider that those outside the four walls of the church are regarded as the others.

Consequently, there exists a perception (again, fairly or unfairly) that being part of a conversation about taking hands with the others, in an effort to make a positive impact on the cities and communities where the church is located, is not necessarily high on the agenda of the weekly gathering of the local church.

The slowness and reluctance in the responses of church leaders when approached to come alongside community efforts and engage in conversation, or even participate with other stakeholders in community impacting projects, may appear, to the uninformed observer, as a lack of concern for what is happening outside the church walls. Being a pastor myself, I am aware how busy the life of a church leader may become depending on the day and the circumstances. So often fatigued, burnt out, under resourced and underpaid church leaders are invited to the table of dialogue by (with respect) organisations and individuals whose situations are far more comfortable and secure - their diaries not half filled with the daily exposure that the pastor experiences as far as the lostness, brokenness and pain of people are concerned.

On closer examination, one may find that quite the opposite is true about the local church, her leaders and those who worship there. Very often the contribution that is made by the local church goes by unnoticed and, truth be told, that is how the church would prefer it. As our Lord Jesus teaches us, 'but when you do a charitable deed, do not let your left hand know what your right hand is doing[49]'. However, it has to be conceded, that within the ranks of the Church, there are those who have developed extensive marketing strategies around their charitable deeds, perhaps with the noble intention of making the necessary impression on the donors and contributors. Nevertheless, when the hour came, the local church was left with little choice. As the lockdown that was imposed on the nation (as in the rest of the world) began to takes its toll on the poorest of the poor, the hungry backyard and shack dwellers came out of their homes and into the streets. The local church (as well as other individuals) had to do their good work out in the open.

If the need was on the streets, then that is where one would find the local church during the horrors of lockdown. The extended hands and feet of God reaching out, giving from very meagre resources to those in greater need than themselves. Feeding, cleaning and clothing their neighbours while they were waiting for promised help that seemed not to be forthcoming. In spite of the threat of prosecution by those who made the promises and were very slow in the execution of those promises, the church took to the streets where the need was and there she served until she had no more to give. Although locked out of her sanctuaries and places of worship, the Church, it seemed, was not sitting idly at home. She was where and when it mattered the most - where the need was. The Church was alive and well and on the move. Nothing was going to stop her now. This is who the Church is.

Chapter 13
THE CHURCH TAKES TO THE STREETS

'Jesus replied, "They do not need to go away.
You give them something to eat."'
Matthew 14:6 (New International Version)

The only constant is change. Outside the church walls, the world was changing and changing at a rapid pace - even before Coronavirus, COVID-19 and lockdown. On the one hand, in the name of progress, the world was moving from revolution to revolution, through the Industrial, Digital, and Information Revolutions to what is now termed the Fourth Industrial Revolution. Then, on the other hand, there are those stubborn facts that militate against this so-called progress, including, but not limited to the impact of poverty, unemployment and inequality. The Church was facing the continued challenge to remain relevant and effective in this fast changing environment. Just when the Church was ready to come out of the building and into the streets, she was unceremoniously told to not only leave the building, but also to remain indoors and stay off the streets as well – like everyone else.

The Church was told in no uncertain terms, 'you are not an essential service'. Pray for the faithful over the phone. Comfort and counsel them over the phone. Preach to them using the social networks. Even if you have obtained a permit to deliver a food parcel, keep your social distance when you interact with church members and no laying on of hands - even with protective clothing. Much of this made perfect sense and sounded completely reasonable, given the circumstances, but how to regulate the care and compassion of people for their fellow humans?

Hungry South Africans were not going to stay indoors and starve to death quietly. As hunger took over and instincts kicked in, they took to the streets. Hundreds of them, who otherwise and under different conditions, would most probably never have displayed the criminal intentions and actions that were demonstrated. Pictures were flooding the media and social networks of supermarket trucks being stopped and robbed by hungry mobs. All the rules and regulations of social distancing and touching went out of the window as people jostled each other for something to eat. Elsewhere angry residents were on the streets for a different reason - they were protesting about the unfair distribution of food parcels. Under these conditions, who was going to keep the foot soldiers of the Church off the streets?

What happened next was unbelievable. Those who were trying to help their fellow humans were warned that they could be acting contrary with the law. The dignity of people still had to be respected even if they were in need of food. Who could be blamed, when arriving with a truckload of food, if a crowd far too big for the delivery appears out of nowhere, almost fighting each other, literally begging not be overlooked? The government responded with even stricter regulations by declaring themselves the sole providers of food to the poor. This, in spite of lacking the capacity of getting it to the hungry masses on an urgent basis and ostensibly out of concern that the virus will spread faster among the people because of a lack of social distancing.[50]

Churches and non-government organisations were warned to comply. No more feeding the poor and hungry. On Sunday, 17 May 2020, the headline in one paper exclaimed, 'Thousands go hungry - yet the rules are even stricter![51]' The article details the reaction of local churches and other organisations to these unexplainable acts of bureaucracy by government. How long should a hungry person wait before he or she is at risk of illness or potential death due to hunger? And when one is

43

already searching for scraps to eat in garbage cans and on refuse heaps, what dignity will be taken away from such an individual when, in an act of compassion and concern, they are offered a meal to eat? Amid the crisis of hunger, things seemed to be moving from the sublime to the ridiculous to the bizarre.

There is an old negro spiritual that goes more or less like this, 'If I can help somebody as I pass along, if I can cheer somebody with a word or a song, if I can show a fellow traveller he is travelling wrong, then my living shall not be in vain.' The Church, as it would be proved under the stress and pressures of lockdown and the devastation that the Coronavirus would unleash on the community, through her own actions and efforts, by virtue of her extended hands and feet, was definitely not falling short in the aspects of helping, encouraging and cheering. What this author is not sure of is whether the silence of the Church, for example, on matters like the food fiasco meant that she regarded the president and his command council on COVID-19 as fellow travellers that were at no part of the journey travelling wrong.

Chapter 14
THE DISCIPLESHIP MOVEMENT

'Students are not greater than their teacher. But the student
who is fully trained will become like the teacher.'
Luke 6:40 (New Living Translation)

Over the last decade or so, in the Church of our Lord Jesus Christ, there has been a renewed interest and focus on the aspect of discipleship. An entire discipleship movement has exploded over the internet and on social media networks. Everywhere, within the church community, this has been welcomed as a very positive development. At last, there is a movement that could get the Church out from within the confines of four walls and into the streets or, as is it is often described, into the market place. For the longest time, this task of getting a significant number of the faithful involved in the great commission of the Church has not been easy. Now, it seems, on an increasing scale, believers are becoming more willing and more comfortable to share their faith with others in their various social circles.

There is not only renewed interest in the aspects of evangelism and discipleship, but also a new excitement on the part of church members to give meaningful expression to their faith by sharing it with family, friends and colleagues in a non-offensive manner. For these interested individuals there are many online training and empowerment opportunities available in this regard. As things stand right now, an increasing number of believers are undergoing some or other type of discipleship training. If one would type the word discipleship into a search engine on the internet, it could be expected that there will be more than 18 million possible entries on offer. It is possible that right about now someone might be asking, but what exactly is a disciple?

The following definition more or less captures the import of the word disciple, 'A disciple is a person who is a devoted follower (pupil, student, apprentice) and believes in the ideas and principles of someone and tries to live the way that person lives or lived and assists in spreading the teachings and doctrines of that person.' A reasonable follow up question may then be asked, but why discipleship? Why all the hype? Why all the training and all the training manuals? For what purpose are all the so-called disciples being trained? What result does all the training have in mind? To use the disciples' own kind of language, what is the mission or mandate? The answer to that question, of course, is that it is a direct instruction, perhaps long neglected, of our Lord Jesus Christ himself in the 28th chapter of Matthew's gospel.[52]

By and large, with some exceptions, the practices and methodologies that the Church has been using since time immemorial have not really proved to be very effective in making disciples who are committed and devoted followers of our Lord Jesus Christ. Those who love those that are lost, bruised and broken and are also passionate about making other disciples. Yet, in spite of this, in the last 100 years one of the amazing miracles of our time has happened right here on the African continent.[53] We are told that, in the beginning of the 1900s, only approximately 10% of the continent was Christian. A century later, after the year 2000, over 50% of Africans were Christian, a growth rate almost unparalleled in any region of the world. Right now, the largest percentage of the world's Christians live on the African continent.[54] However, are all of them disciples?

46

A fact that should not be overlooked is that the world's two major religions both have a growth strategy or spiritual empire building mandate within their Holy Scriptures - to go and make disciples of all people, everywhere. We have also been made aware that according to current research, within the next 30 to 40 years, Christians might no longer be the majority religion in the world. Why would this be the case? A lack of discipleship perhaps? In life, some opportunities come to us. These should be grabbed with enthusiasm and urgency. It would be foolish to ignore or miss a chance or an opportunity that comes to you, presented on a silver platter, in a manner of speaking.

The same is true of so-called opportunities for growth. Like other kinds of opportunities, some are right in front of us and it would be a dereliction of duty to let them pass by. However, not all opportunities just simply present themselves to us. Some require us to go in search of them. However, before we go, we have to prepare ourselves in a way that we have the confidence, character and capacity to maximise those opportunities when we stumble upon them. As someone once said, 'The secret of success is to be ready for your time when it comes.' When the Church looks back on the year 2020, would the challenges presented by the arrival of the Coronavirus and its cousin COVID-19, be regarded as something that the Church experienced as an unfortunate interruption or will we, with hindsight and gratitude, be able to declare that when the opportunity presented itself, the Church was ready for the moment?

Chapter 15
COVID-19 – INTERRUPTION OR OPPORTUNITY?

'Make the most of every opportunity in these evil days.'
Ephesians 5:16 (New Living Translation)

Was the arrival of the coronavirus and COVID-19 an interruption for the Church?

If the founder of a movement is clearly identifiable and that individual has clearly articulated the vision and objectives of the movement, it could be a useful endeavour to compare the current priorities of the movement to that described by the founder, in this case our Lord Jesus Christ himself. Based on the great commission, the Jesus movement is an international, disciple making movement which is supposed to empower and equip its followers to observe all the things that the leader has commanded them to do, including, one could assume, all the things in which the leader himself has set the example.

When one takes a closer look at the content of the command in the 19th verse of the 28th chapter of Matthew's gospel, an important clue is hiding in plain sight. It is the verb 'go' right at the beginning of the sentence. This is a clear indication that Jesus was not only deploying disciples, but also disciples on the move. Not only a gathering every Sunday, but a daily lifestyle of being salt and light to the world out there. They were supposed to be like a city on a hill and like a lamp that provides light to all, touching lives, making a positive difference wherever they went.

It should further also be safe to assume that the teaching of a disciple is not only for the accumulation of knowledge, but rather the beginning of being taught all things with the purpose of the new recruits, in turn, being strategically deployed. In many disciplines, the disciple literally learns from the master through imitating the ways of the master. This include the ways of love and forgiveness, grace and compassion, sharing and caring, bringing hope and good news, walking the extra mile and turning the other cheek. Always ready to serve, towel in hand, living a life of service and sacrifice, regarding the interests of others more important than their own. Imitating the master.

This much is clear. The disciple is not given a range of options to choose from. The great commission, as it is called, is not a suggestion nor is it a request. It is a command. This is no holy huddle. There is no time to hide from the real world by spending our days and nights in the upper room. It seems that God wants us out of our buildings and into the streets. He will even go so far as to send a mighty wind to blow us out of our comfort zones to where the need is - the pain, the hunger, the brokenness, the homelessness, the loneliness and the hopelessness.

There are three well-known examples that Jesus used in the New Testament gospels on how to influence one's environment - light, salt[55] and seed.[56] One can make one's own assumptions about the lessons to be drawn from these, but in essence, there is on the one hand, a very direct and very visible manner in which one can make a difference to one's surroundings - like a candle being lit in a dark room. On the other hand, there is the not so visible effect like salt in food (providing taste without being visible) – tasted, but not seen. Then there is the lesson of the mustard seed - small at first, but big in the end. Therefore, it seems, then, that the approach of the church should not be an either-or approach, but a both-and-more approach.

Have we as church leaders (or some of us) perhaps underestimated the contribution that we are making in our communities and in our cities? Do we perhaps act with this low self-esteem posture on an ongoing basis? Is our contribution under-publicised? Even worse, do we shy away from publication because we, in fact, do undervalue and underrate the impact of our labours? Many of us perform our tasks in under-resourced organisations serving under-resourced communities, sometimes under the most difficult conditions imaginable. What should be our posture if the leader of the movement himself has assured us that the gates of hell will not prevail against us?

We do not know whether God sent the COVID-19 pandemic to teach us a lesson. Although there are those who preach this kind of message (God forbid), this one thing we know - because of COVID-19, the Church has been kicked out of her comfort zone, out of her bricks and mortar. The only drawback is, the Church was not kicked into the streets (that situation would have suited the church ideally), but was sent home to stay home until further notice like everyone else. Suddenly, we had to learn new ways of doing church. Those who were quick on the uptake were beginning to promote the church at home and the church online. Not everyone was that ready, and as with the rest of the population, the impact of the lockdown on the Church and the believers would turn out to be quite wide ranging.

Chapter 16
THE LOCAL CHURCH IS PUSHED ONLINE

'But divide your investments among many places,
for you do not know what risks might lie ahead.'
Ecclesiastes 11:2 (New Living Translation)

I am not sure what it was.

A gut feel, a sense of anticipation, a premonition or a heavenly download.

After watching and listening to the president of South Africa on Sunday, 15 March 2020, I became overwhelmed with a sense of unrelenting urgency that, until today, I cannot fully explain. The next day I scheduled a number of meetings, first with the staff and executive committee and then we invited all the ministry leaders of our local church to a full briefing on Wednesday evening, 18 March 2020.

Another meeting was scheduled for Wednesday, 25 March 2020. We became engaged in a conversation around a discussion document entitled, *The Next 10 Days*. In spite of the fact that we had already paid the full amount for a conference venue and accommodation to attend a strategic planning session of the Governing Body (Church Board), scheduled to take place on the last weekend of March, something inside of me warned me that this was not going to take place,.

I already had a sense that our year plan and all the activities planned therein, as well as our annual budget was in jeopardy. Only 100 members per service? How were we going to do that? On any given Sunday, we would have at least between 800 and 1 000 people in attendance in our morning services. In the end, we took the route of inviting people to six different services based on the first letter of their surnames. The staff, musicians, worship singers and ushers all declared themselves available for a weekend that would last from Saturday to Tuesday - the longest weekend ever! By the grace of God, those six services went off rather well because a third of our regular attendees simply did not turn up, but the tithing income for the weekend dropped by two thirds! Not a good sign. How long would we be able to keep this up?

While we were still planning for the next round of multiple services, the state president dropped the bombshell on 23 March 2020. The country would be going into total lockdown from midnight on 26 March 2020 until 16 April 2020. There would no public gatherings of any kind and any number. Every citizen was warned to stay at home and only leave their homes for essential items like food and chronic medication. No one would be going to work or to the office, except those individuals identified as essential workers. No public gatherings - so no church, no pulpit, no preaching, no worship and, of course, no collection of tithes and offerings. The Church would have to go online. What did that mean? How would our local church reach about 1 000 people online, much less, how would they be able to give the Lord's tithe online? How would the church staff and other expenses be paid?

Our local church did not exactly have an online presence. Others were way ahead of us in this regard. We had a Facebook page that had been going for a year or so where we would post the occasional batch of pictures of our Sunday services. We had a regular photographer and we would, as far possible, post a picture of the Sunday speaker with a summary of his or her message to the believers. That was it. No regular videography, no real live streaming, except individual members posting what they captured on their own private devices.

Until the evening of 23 March 2020, everything we did and the way that we did it was focused on an audience that was present in a church building every Sunday.

During early January, our son, Joshua, used his life's savings to buy himself a new camera. His Mom and I were not as excited as he was about the idea. As far as we were concerned, the camera that he already owned was not a bad camera at all. However, we agreed, and after the purchase, he started showing us regularly how superior the quality of his new camera was, compared to his older one. Not only the picture quality, but also especially the quality of the videography. It was with this camera that on Saturday evening, 21 March 2020, he would record the first of our six services for posterity. It was a very modest start and any observant viewer, having regard to the quality of the recording, would easily pick up that that it was probably our first attempt. However, it was a good practice run, which would stand us in good stead in the days and weeks to come.

Chapter 17
THE CHURCH IN THE TOWNSHIP

'The rich man's wealth is his strong city; The destruction
of the poor is their poverty.'
Proverbs 10:15 (New King James Version)

In South Africa, when we speak of the nation's three biggest
challenges, we will usually refer to the evil triplets of poverty, inequality
and unemployment.[57] When the coronavirus reached our shores, a
very harsh light would be cast on these evil triplets and expose the
enormous gap that existed between the haves and the have-nots.
Very often the issues of race and class are intricately woven into the
fabric of South African life where making a living in a township is very
different from life in the suburbs. Usually, the evil triplets resided in the
townships. The township is what the majority of South Africa's poor
and unemployed call home. It makes sense that a church in the
township will be significantly under resourced when compared to a
well-resourced church in the leafy suburbs. It so happens that I am a
pastor of a church in a township.

Within the first two weeks of the lockdown, the differences would
become known. The income in the poorer churches dropped
dramatically precipitating an almost immediate financial crisis at the
end of March 2020. In the suburbs, pastors were reporting a slight
drop in income - between ten and twenty percent, while the poorer
churches had a drop in income of between 40% and 80%. The
reason? The faithful in the township brought their tithes and offering to
church on Sundays - almost all in cash. Very little or no use was made
of the banks' electronic channels. It would be a devastating blow, first
in the household of the pastor and his family and then, of course, for
the members of those churches. The same would be true for being

54

able to stay in touch with the faithful via online ministry during the period of lockdown.

Very often, with few exceptions, at the very least, a church in the suburbs would have a full time staff complement of 10 or more people. In addition, there would be teams of individuals in place specialising in worship and hospitality, as well as a multimedia team. The responsibilities of these multimedia teams would include sound, visuals and making sure the church had an online presence if not through a TV channel, then through social networks or both. On the other hand, in township churches, with few exceptions, there would not be any significant investment in an online ministry. Many pastors found the mixed impact and mixed results rather confusing - how could life continue almost normally in churches in the suburbs while in the townships there could be such devastation?

The answer was not too complicated. For a long time the faithful in the suburbs had been making their financial contributions through the banks' electronic channels and the impact on their income and livelihoods had, it seemed, been less severe than on those households in the township. So, when the Church went online during lockdown, it soon became clear that the church in the suburbs largely were in a greater state of readiness than most churches in the township. This could be seen in the quality of the footage, as well as the content and structure of the online presentation. Still, township pastors have to be admired for their willingness to work with what they had. They would use their own personal cell phones to deliver their sermons to their members and sometimes would cut short their messages because of a shortage of data.

While our local church had a Facebook page that has been running since late 2018, our online presence was a very modest presence, to say the least. As far as the production capacity for live streaming was concerned, we were relatively inexperienced. Up to the announcement of the lockdown, we had not yet produced a single video recording. To say it would be a steep learning curve would really be an understatement. As inexperienced as countries and governments were in handling the onslaught of the coronavirus, so inexperienced was our team as far as having regular church services online was concerned. Nevertheless, at the very least, we had to try it. My son, a second year university student, stuck at home, was very willing to assist us in this regard. We were going to give it our best shot - trying to reach about a thousand of our church members online.

None of the team members involved in the production of our church online videos could have imagined what would follow in the weeks to come. To our complete surprise (shock would perhaps be a better word), not only would we reach our own members through online ministry, but also an entire new audience would join in on the social networks - tens and tens of thousands of them. Not only was our township church reaching more people in our own city, but thousands of people all over the world. On the other hand, we were very much aware that as far as the township church was concerned with regard to online reach, our story would be the exception rather than the rule. Church members in the township just simply did not have the capacity or access to the required resources like airtime or data.

Chapter 18
A CITY, INTERRUPTED

'For when they say, "Peace and safety!" then sudden destruction
comes upon them, as labour pains upon a pregnant woman.
And they shall not escape.'
1 Thessalonians 5:3 (New King James Version)

I love my city.

I have lived in Cape Town for all of my 60 years. About one million people live in the immediate vicinity of the central business district, but more than four million[58] live in the greater metropolitan area. The city has been named the best place in the world to visit by both *The New York Times*[59] and *The Daily Telegraph*.[60] Visitors fall in love with the rolling wine lands and our majestic Table Mountain, surrounded by the most beautiful beaches. Having had the privilege to visit many global cities, I understand why visitors appreciate the scenic beauty of our city. On my travels I have seen many cities with much to view and appreciate, but few as lovely as our city's beautiful locations. On the other hand, Cape Town is also known as the most violent city in South Africa and has recently been ranked as the 11th most violent city in the world.[61]

There are also many positive prophecies about the city of Cape Town. For the longest time now, there has been the prophecy that a fire of revival will start at the southern tip of Africa and spread across South Africa and to the rest of the continent of Africa. In addition to this perennial prophecy, many other prophecies have been recorded that God is up to something in the city of Cape Town, which will affect the entire continent of Africa. As if in response to the prophecies, over the last few years, many local and international gospel movements have become active in the city. In this regard, many city impacting events have taken place and continue to take place in the city of Cape Town. This response by movements and their leaders to the prophecies is probably an indication that the prophecies are being taken seriously.

During the month of May 2019, our city was host to two Pan African conferences. In the first week, the New York based organisation, movement.org, hosted leaders from about 25 African cities who reflected on how gospel movements can be mobilised in all African cities. Towards the end of May, Global Teen Challenge Africa hosted a conference where leaders from 28 African countries grappled with the scourge of substance abuse facing the continent. I had the God given privilege to speak very briefly at both of these events. These happy coincidences should not be underestimated. Think about it. Between these events, leaders from 50 African countries gathered in our city about how we can make a difference - in our city, on the continent and beyond.

However, like other cities of the world, our city too, was rudely interrupted by the arrival of COVID-19. Not many months after the outbreak in Wuhan, China, the first so-called epicentre of infection and death due to the coronavirus, the city of Cape Town would become the so-called epicentre of South Africa. On 20 May 2020, an article in the *Washington Post*[62] explained why this was the case. According to the article, South African epidemiologists were curious how the virus was spreading so fast in our city while the rest of the continent of Africa had largely escaped the waves of death. Apparently one of the main reasons why this was the case was that, up to very late in March, the city welcomed more tourists from hard hit regions of the world than the rest of Africa.

City leaders, with the help of medical experts, had identified a number of hotspots in the city where the rate of infection and deaths was higher than elsewhere in the city. According to the same *Washington Post* article, the super spreading of the coronavirus was taking place in two main centres where most of the residents were working class people. The areas that were identified was Tygerberg and Khayelitsha. Almost two months earlier, one of the city's daily newspapers had warned that the virus had already made its appearance in Khayelitsha and the other densely populated township, Mitchells Plain.[63] And because about two thirds of the country's infections and deaths due to the virus were in Cape Town, all eyes were on the city and many were wondering aloud whether the city should not be kept on a higher alert level[64] than the rest of the country.

It was being estimated that at the height of the infection rate, our city would be near 80 000[65] infections. A shortage of available hospital beds was predicted and already the infection rate was increasing amongst those working on the frontline. At one city hospital, more than 100 nurses and staff were tested positive for the virus.[66] Being the epicentre of the coronavirus in the country was, however, not the only problem that the city was facing. On a number of fronts, a range of other challenges was presenting themselves.

Chapter 19
TROUBLE IN THE CITY OF CAPE TOWN

'Pray to me in time of trouble.
I will rescue you, and you will honour me.'
Psalm 50:15 (Common English Version)

Within less than a month after the South African nation went into lockdown, there were 22 confirmed deaths[67] in our city and it was anticipated that at the peak of the outbreak, the city of Cape Town would experience more than 80 000 infections of the coronavirus with a concomitant shortage of 1 000 beds for new patients. Concerns were already raised at the end of March when COVID-19 infections reached the two biggest communities in the city, namely Khayelitsha and Mitchells Plain where a combined population of about three quarter of a million people lived in some of the poorest conditions in the city.

As was the case in many cities of the world, the other challenges that had to be addressed was the matter of the homeless people living in our city. This was not going to be an easy task and the relocation of the homeless to alternative places of accommodation later became one of the city's biggest headaches. This was due to a hopelessly short timeline allowed for planning and preparation. In the end, more division was created in an already divided city where the gap between the rich and the poor is a glaring reality. The headlines in the local papers shouted it out, 'City divided over homeless[68]' and 'COVID-19: A tale of two cities[69]'.

One very poorly managed relocation of homeless individuals was to a place on the coast where they were to be housed in a tent on a sports field. Later dubbed a concentration camp,[70] it brought along with it a lot of negative publicity for the city. In the wisdom of the mayor and other church leaders in the city, an open-air church service was held just outside the camp for the benefit of those in the camp. A move criticised by other church leaders in the city, which led to division even within the ranks of the Church. In addition, after a less than positive report by Doctors Without Borders (MSF),[71] the continued existence of the camp became untenable for the city and it was closed down.

There are many organisations and individuals in our city who are doing amazing work as far as promoting the unity and wellbeing of all the citizens of our city is concerned. I have been blessed with the good fortune of working with these amazing leaders who, in my opinion, are true servants in the Kingdom of God and who love and serve our city with commitment and much humility. For years now, we have been collaborating across denominations, taking hands with business as well as community leaders. It is hard work that comes along with a lot of criticism. A lot of patience, tenacity and perseverance is required to stay the course.

Therefore, when the coronavirus and COVID-19 reached the shores of Cape Town, everybody pitched in. All the gospel city movements, including prayer movements and other city impacting initiatives began to consider ways and means on how to best respond to the situation at hand. On the one hand, there was the "concentration camp" where the treatment of the homeless was threatening to cause division even within our own ranks and on the other, there was the growing problem of vulnerable families going without food and the very slow movement on the part of government to bring relief to these destitute families.

As critically important as these two situations were, and as much as they were screaming out for a response and an intervention, it is the humble view of this author that it would consume so much time, effort

61

and energy, that the plight of church leaders, in particular, as well as church members were not receiving the attention they deserved. After Church gatherings were banned for almost two months, there was need and hunger, even in the homes of pastors, especially those who lived and ministered in poor communities. In my own denomination (within the Western Cape region), we had to come to the aid of the households of more than 20 pastors and their families. We were helping everybody else while our own were suffering.

It is probably at this point that I realised I was finding it hard to appreciate the pre-occupation of my fellow labourers, whom I love so dearly, with prayer and food parcels. This, while we seemed to be in full support of government keeping the church doors shut. At the very least, we were not protesting nearly half as much as the taxi industry did with so much success. Neither did we come close to the amount of trouble taken by the tobacco industry[72] or the entertainment industry.[73] To this author it seemed as if the Church was in full agreement with government that a 35% or 50% filled church building would pose a much bigger health risk than a 70% filled taxi. Maybe, one day, with the benefit of hindsight, it might be revealed that there would have been no greater risk to church members than to taxi commuters. Again, it dawned on me that on these matters as well, there was not complete agreement within our own ranks.

Chapter 20
THE CHURCH AND THE CITY

'And when He drew near and saw the city, he wept over it...'
Luke 19:41 (English Standard Version)

The Scriptures make it clear that God loves people everywhere and He prefers that none should perish.[74] That is the very reason that God sent His only Son to seek and to save those who are lost. People who live in the most rural and most remote parts of our world, like city dwellers, are deeply loved by their Creator. Those who live and labour amongst them should be remembered in all our prayers and be applauded for their willingness and determination to render their service under such conditions. In many places, the challenges of the city are moving over to the rural areas. In my own city, the crime lords and the drug lords are expanding their businesses into the rural areas at an alarming rate. The difference between the city and rural reality is the sheer scale of the city dynamic compared to the rural.

It has been said that the Bible story starts in a garden and ends in a city.

Actually, from Genesis to Revelation a few hundred places are referred to as cities. Some are more well-known than others, to name a few in alphabetical order - Alexandra, Antioch, Athens, Babel, Babylon, Bethlehem, Jericho, Jerusalem, Rome as well as the towns of Sodom and Gomorrah. The towns of Sodom and Gomorrah, in particular, are known for their hedonism and decadent lifestyles, and, as we learn, the very reason why God destroyed the two cities.

In the Bible there are many other references to cities, too many to record here. Many of those cities mentioned above still exist today. To

63

name only a few, Babylon (now Baghdad), Athens, Rome and Jerusalem - the city that made Jesus weep. Speaking of Babylon, there is a lesson in the message that God sent to the exiles through the prophet Jeremiah. God told them to work towards the peace and prosperity of Babylon. From the fruit of their own labour, they too would enjoy peace and prosperity.

So, it seems then, that while the ancient cities were probably very different in architecture and character when compared to our contemporary cities, as the social ills prevailed during that day, so now, in our day, our own cities face their own present day challenges. The scope of these challenges are many and wide ranging - from poverty, inequality, education, housing, health and safety to environmental challenges like the scarcity of natural resources, technology, infrastructure, economic development and good governance.

These stubborn realities have a significant impact on the world's cities and on those who live and work in these cities. Very often, what may be regarded as the least of these challenges, like the availability of natural resources may overnight become the major challenge facing a city. A case in point is Cape Town, South Africa, the city that I have called home for more than sixty years. Over the last few years, the city has experienced a severe drought. So severe that, for a while, almost everyone wondered aloud whether Cape Town would be the first city in the world to run out of water.[75]

Not only environmental factors like climate change that affects our cities. There is also the explosive population growth over the last two decades. It is estimated that about two billion people have been added to the planet over the last two decades. Fast forward to the year 2050 and imagine what the picture would like then. We are told that already

64

the majority of the world's population are living in our cities and that in the next 30 years this could increase to as much as 80%.[76]

As the world changes, so will our cities. It is predicted that by the end of this century, of the present 10 most populated cities in the world, only two will be counted amongst the top ten. At present, only one African city, namely Cairo is counted amongst the ten most populated cities of the world, in the new scenario it is predicted that the majority of the world's most populated cities will be African cities. It is estimated that by 2100, between 50 million and 90 million people will be living in each of these cities - the majority in Africa.

All over the planet, people are leaving the rural areas in ever-increasing numbers and they are moving to the world's cities. Depending on whom one is talking to the number of people currently residing in the world's cities may range from 50% to 60% of the global population. As already mentioned, it is further predicted that over the next 30 years well over two thirds of the world's population would be living in cities. Most, if not all, of these travellers believe that they are moving to a better life for themselves and their families.

Chapter 21
IN SEARCH OF A BETTER LIFE?

'I observed everything going on under the sun,
and really, it is all meaningless - like chasing the wind.'
Ecclesiastes 1:14 (New Living Translation)

All over the world, the movement towards cities continues unabated.

As mentioned in the previous chapter, our world is becoming urbanised. If some studies are anything to go by, there appears to be an acceleration as we approach the third decade of the twenty-first century. It seems that about 60 years ago (1960)[77] only one third of the world population were residing in cities. Currently, that figure stands at more than half and according to most predictions, by the end of the twenty-first century, more than two thirds of global citizens (as already stated in the previous chapter) will be living in cities. Some put the figure as high as 80%.

This rapid growth is driven by both the new birth rate, an exodus from the world's rural areas, as well as conflict and natural disasters. In most cases, people leave the places where their ancestors lived for generations with the hope that they will be able to live a better life in the cities. This not only increases the pressure on the resources of the cities, but also on the capacity to provide the services that these new citizens would require, including housing and sanitation, employment, education and access to healthcare.

Percentages is one thing, but when one looks at the actual numbers being predicted for global urban growth, it can be quite staggering. It is estimated that by the year 2050 the world population could stand at about 10 billion people of which close to seven billion will be living in the cities of the world. It is hard to begin to imagine the socio-economic and socio-political challenges that will come along with this enormous coming together in the cities on our planet. If one also keeps in mind that a significant number of these city dwellers will be poor, undereducated and unemployed, the dynamic changes dramatically.

An exponential increase in urban growth unavoidably leads to overcrowding, which in turn leads to the creation and proliferation of informal settlements. The number of people living in these so-called informal settlements directly influences the measurement of living standards in urban populations. A household in an informal settlement may be described as a group of people living under the same roof lacking one or more of the following conditions: access to improved water, access to improved sanitation, sufficient living area and durability of housing. This creates fertile ground for many social ills of which the continued cycle of poverty leads the way.

It makes sense that the institutions, who are burdened with the responsibility of providing the essential services that are required for these human beings to spend their lives in conditions that are conducive to their wellbeing, face a formidable task. Governments, semi-government institutions, business and the nonprofit sector (including the Church) continue the struggle to forge meaningful partnerships, given the very different nature and character of the organisations that are committed to make a difference in the lives of these individuals.

A fair question might be, as things stand at present, is the Church (as part of the nonprofit sector) making a meaningful contribution towards the solutions or at least actively participating in the efforts towards finding the solutions to these tremendously difficult challenges facing global citizens? If the answer to this question is a yes, is it at all possible to quantify the contribution of the Church? Is it perhaps possible that, in the most poverty stricken parts of our world, under-resourced individuals and organisations are making a contribution that requires only a strategic boost through recognition of their work and the provision of resources to catapult their efforts to the next level?

This changing environment presents a challenge to church leaders who live and minister in the cities. The situation begs for an entirely new approach to doing church in the city. As Alvin Toffler might put it, 'we have to learn new ways of doing things through unlearning the old and then relearning new ways of doing things[78]'.

The influx of new people into our cities brings along with it many new challenges. There is the pressure on the city's resources and the potential for conflict when it is perceived that there is not equal access for all the new city dwellers to the city's resources. Differences in language and culture add to a situation that requires new thinking and a new approach to the management of a contemporary city. One thing leads to another and next the lack of employment opportunities leads to joblessness, gangsterism, crime, substance abuse and teenage pregnancies, to name a few. However, hidden within this dark picture are many opportunities for the Church to minister to the lost, the hurt, the broken and the destitute.

Clearly, under these circumstances, and beyond COVID-19, in the cities of the world, it can no longer be church as usual. Even if that sounds like a cliché, the need to learn new skills, new methods and new ways of engaging different people from different backgrounds has increased exponentially. Working as a team member in diverse groups of people outside one's usual leadership role requires a complete reorientation in both thinking and attitude. This calls for great humility and a willingness to serve and not be served. In my home city of Cape Town, many church buildings that were once standing empty are now filled to capacity with vibrant and enthusiastic worshippers. In many cases these worshippers turn out be new city dwellers! However, COVID-19 will have an effect on the way we do church for some time to come.

Chapter 22
CONCERN FOR THE LOCAL CHURCH

'Then, besides all this, I have the daily burden of
my concern for all the churches.'
2 Corinthians 11:28 (New Living Translation)

One of the most undeserved graces that has been bestowed on me in life is that, in addition to my duties as presiding pastor of our local church, I also happen to be the leader of about 50 more churches in our city. There are many others with greater distinction who could probably step into my shoes at any time. Until then, God, in His wisdom, seems to have decided that it is my responsibility. One single pastor leads some of these churches and others have multiple pastoral staff. In total, just over 90 pastors serving 50 local churches. Many of these great servants of God work in very poor areas and serve communities that are significantly under resourced, to say the least. So, when the announcement of lockdown was made on 23 March 2020, I called an urgent meeting with the leaders of these 50 churches on 25 March 2020, the day before lockdown.

Aware that in the coming days, our freedom of movement would be restricted and meetings of such a nature would be out of the question for at least three weeks, we huddled together to discuss ways and means of staying in touch with each other, as well as with those entrusted to our spiritual care. During the conversation that followed, a few things became clear. None of us was really prepared for what was waiting up ahead. The time available before the lockdown would kick in was just not enough to put in place all the necessary arrangements to stay in touch with the members of the church and perform our duties by remote means such as social networks and other online means. While we were considering what the possible impact might be

70

on our local churches during the period of lockdown, one specific possibility became a huge cause for concern.

Not only would it be difficult to minister to the spiritual needs of the flock from a distance, there would almost certainly be a significant financial impact on the members of the church and, as a consequence on the income of the church. At this point, it might be helpful to the reader to explain the financial model and structure within our own denomination. There is a decentralised financial system. Each local church is responsible to generate its own income, acquire or rent its own assets, including places of worship and other assets. The local church, while retaining 90% of its income, is responsible to pay about a tenth of its income to the next higher structure. The downside to this decentralised model is that some churches are less resourced than others are and, in the churches located in the poorer neighbourhoods, there are an ongoing struggle to make ends meet.

It was anticipated that the churches in the more affluent neighbourhoods would probably also be affected by the lockdown, but not half as much as those in the townships. Over the last few years, the significant part of the income of these churches in the suburbs would be received via electronic means, with the majority of members making use of digital banking channels. Quite the opposite was happening in the townships, where a strong cash economy is the order of the day. I could sense the apprehension of my colleagues while they wondered about what the potential impact would be when the church members would no longer be bringing their cash tithing contributions to God's storehouse[79] every Sunday, a tradition that goes back many generations. While we pondered about the possibilities that might manifest itself over the following three months, the actual effect would prove to be far more devastating than any of us could ever imagined.

71

Some churches were very fortunate and experienced an average reduction of somewhere between 10% and 30% of their monthly income for the period March to May 2020, but those churches that were the worst hit lost up to 70% of their monthly tithing income. There was a combination of reasons for this state of affairs. The first reason was that many of the breadwinners and income earners in these poor households were suddenly not receiving any income at all. The second was the fact that many members simply were not used to giving their tithes by electronic means. Thirdly, very few of the churches that had been affected negatively were able to communicate effectively with their members because of inadequate record keeping of their members' contact details.

Nevertheless, they were part of the family and in desperate need of assistance. Having been warned by the apostle Paul that those who do not look after their own should be considered as worse than unbelievers should, we fully understood what the right thing was to do. It was time for those who were in a stronger position to come to the aid of those who were in a weaker position.[80] We had to respond to the devastation that had struck about a third of our pastors' households.

Chapter 23
AFRICA – THE NEW EPICENTRE OF THE DISEASE?

'A fool will believe anything...'
Proverbs 14:15a (Good News Translation)

During mid-April 2020, the WHO issued a warning that Africa could become the next epicentre[81] of the COVID-19 outbreak. This, in spite of the fact that at the time of writing, Africa had in the vicinity of only 74 000 confirmed cases, more than 26 000 recoveries and only about 2 500 deaths out of a population of about 1.3 billion people. In the same article, nameless officials from the United Nations (UN) were predicting that the pandemic will kill at least 300 000 people in Africa and push nearly 30 million into poverty. Apparently, in the week before the warning was issued there had been a sharp rise of coronavirus cases in Africa. The UN Economic Commission for Africa called for a one billion dollar safety net for the continent, including the halting of external debt payments.

It seemed that the warning issued by the World Health Organisation was based on a number of concerns. First was the trend that the spread of the virus was taking on the continent - it appeared to be spreading away from Africa's capital cities. Secondly was the concern that there were not enough ventilators in Africa to deal with the pandemic. Thirdly was the fact that more than a third of the continent's population lacked access to adequate water supplies and nearly 60% of urban dwellers lived in overcrowded slums - ideal conditions for the virus to spiral out of control. Most of the deaths on the continent, at the time of writing, was in Algeria and South Africa.

However, long before the arrival of COVID-19, the attention of the global community had been on Africa. The reasons for this are many and varied and most of them have to do with, amongst other, the stubborn and persistent challenges of poverty, conflict and displacement of people from their land of birth. Consequently, the negative effects on all the people who live on the continent, particularly women and children. Then, during 2018, a study conducted by the Centre for the Study of Global Christianity at Gordon-Conwell Theological Seminary revealed that more than 631 million Christians[82] were presently living on African soil, close to half of the continent's population. This was more than good news. Percentage wise, the continent of Africa was home to more Christians than any other continent.

In addition, we are told that the biggest move towards cities is happening in Africa. At the last count, only one of the top 10 biggest cities in the world was in Africa. All of that is apparently about to change, not too long from now. It is predicted that by 2025 at least 100 African cities[83] will be home to more than one million people. Apparently, in just over a decade, the city of Lagos will grow by about 8 million people. By the end of the twenty-first century, the majority of world citizens will be living in African cities. Imagine living in a city where you have more than 80 million neighbours. Imagine the pressure on the city administration and other relevant institutions that are responsible to cater for the needs of so many citizens. If some of the prophecies over the continent of Africa are to be taken seriously, then, in spite of COVID-19, it seems that the rest of Africa's days will be the best of her days.

If one particular prophecy[84] is anything to go by then, it seems, Africa's immediate future does not look bleak at all. According to this prophecy, Africa will be coming out of years of wars and poverty, and there will be a radical change in government and politics. Africa will begin to lead the world in innovative discoveries. The prophecy continues that a greater unity within Africa will come and even crime, which has benefited greatly from the continent's resources, will be turned around. The prophecy concluded with the words, 'the Lord has heard the cries of His people there and will turn this injustice around'. Now, this type of prophecy has been criticised in the past and the reader might benefit from some insights in a piece written by a certain Marius Nel.[85]

The question may be asked, why Africa? Perhaps because God is really up to something on our continent. Not something small or insignificant, but something that will change the trajectory of Africa for the good and for good. The signs are already here. All roads are leading to Africa. Everybody is coming to Africa. God uses people and God works through leaders. This author will not be surprised if, right at this present moment, God is perhaps already preparing his chosen instruments that He is ready to deploy for the new bloodless revolution in Africa - a revolution of hope and prosperity. More than just the so-called African Renaissance or the New African Dawn, but by the grace of God, a life changing, sustainable, total transformation of the African continent. Meanwhile, at the height of the COVID-19 pandemic, something was happening just off the east coast of Africa. Was the prophecy of innovation coming from the continent being fulfilled or not? Moreover, lest we forget, a good relationship exists between our Lord and the continent of Africa. When His life was threatened during His very early years on earth, Africa gave Him refuge.

Chapter 24
MADAGASCAR AND THE VIRUS

'"Nazareth!" exclaimed Nathanael. "Can anything
good come from Nazareth?"'
John 1:46 (New Living Translation)

Can something good come out of Africa?

At the time of writing, the African continent had about 120 000
confirmed cases[86] of the coronavirus of whom about 50 000 people
had recovered with less than 4 000 deaths recorded. About 400
kilometres off the East African coast lies the island country of
Madagascar. According to Wikipedia, Madagascar, officially the
Republic of Madagascar, and previously known as the Malagasy
Republic, at 592 800km^2, is the world's second largest island country
with a population of about 26 million people. As at 28 May 2020, the
country had 612 confirmed cases[87] of the COVID-19 of whom 151
patients had recovered and only two deaths were recorded.

The island country has been in the news since declaring that they may
have stumbled on a miracle cure for the COVID-19 pandemic. It is in
the form of a bottled herbal mixture of which the main ingredient is
Artemisia, a plant that is indigenous to China. After being imported
from China in the 1970s it is now widely grown on the island,
according to an article written on 11 May 2020.[88] Apparently, the plant
has proved its usefulness in the treatment of malaria. According to the
same article, Madagascar's president, Andry Rajoelina, has
suggested that the herbal tea gives results within seven days, based
on tests that have been conducted. The president has not only
admitted to taking the medicine personally, but has even taken a drink
in full view of the public.

It is further understood that South Africa has expressed willingness to assist Madagascar with the scientific analysis of the drink, known as Covid Organics. South Africa's minister of health, Zweli Mkhize, in a Twitter post,[89] confirmed this. Apparently, South African scientists would be assisting only with the scientific analysis of the herb. However, not everyone has responded warmly to the claims made by the Madagascan president. Amongst them was Shabir Madhi,[90] as well as the World Health Organisation, who in all reasonableness, requested access to the testing methods that were used in leading the good president and his team of experts to come to their conclusions that their drink was a cure for the COVID-19 disease.

Time will tell whether the island country of Madagascar, like so many before them, was offering another fake concoction to the world, in the name of a cure. Alternatively, as so many times before, another opportunity might be lost to the African continent to share a much more affordable solution to a crisis than the world's capitalists always have in mind. There seems to be a perennial perception out there that in Africa we are inherently incompetent and corrupt. That people from other nations are not as corrupt as, and much more competent than we are. Africans, for a while now, have been receiving unsolicited training and development opportunities, travelling opportunities, even free books, seminars and webinars, but not necessarily cash for worthy projects. The statistics about the impact of COVID-19, however, tell a very different story about the competent management of the crisis by many world leaders outside of Africa.

There are many more instances where Africa has proved to the world that the continent has more to offer the global family, too many to record here. Take for example the fact that, currently, the highest percentage of Christians are to be found on the African continent - more than 631 million Christians, about 45% of the continent's population. If the success is in Africa, does it not imply that the recipe for the success is also in Africa? Does this not mean that the wisdom to this success also emanates from Africa? Should this wisdom not be exported, distributed to and shared by Africans with the world? Should the content of the materials, based on this wisdom, not feel, look and sound like it originated in Africa? If the materials do not feel, look and sound like Africa, where is the source of its origin? If the materials did not originate in Africa, why is it offered to and in Africa?

If foreign (or western) material is not achieving similar success elsewhere, is it unreasonable of Africans to be suspicious about not only the materials, but also the motivation of the distributors of those materials? If there are things to learn from Africans, why must Africans be led by those who ostensibly want to learn from us? Why are Africans not the ones leading, empowering and educating in the field of their success?

A pity that at the time of writing, the final story of Madagascar's Covid Organics has not been told. I hope it turns out to be another good African story, instead of another credibility setback for the continent.

Chapter 25
MEANWHILE, BACK IN SOUTH AFRICA

'Without good advice everything goes wrong - it takes
careful planning for things to go right.'
Proverbs 15:22 (Contemporary English Version)

Back in South Africa, by the time the nation had already endured more than 50 days of lockdown, the patience of the people was wearing thin. All over the place, individuals and organisations were rising up and making their voices heard. The decisions of the president and his so-called command council were being questioned from within and from without. The ruling party's own were calling some of the lockdown regulations irrational.[91] While it appeared the Church was continuing with either her silence or her invisible behind the scenes consultations (if any) with government, other voices were coming through loud and clear. 'Save South Africa! End lockdown![92]' exclaimed the headline in a Sunday newspaper. In another Sunday newspaper, the editorial column referred to 'the hour of the great storm[93]'.

It was of course, the president himself, who declared in his low content speech of 13 May 2020 that he was in consultations with various stakeholders. However, some of the very individuals and organisations who, in the estimation of the reasonable person, might have been considered stakeholders were calling on the president to disclose all the identities of the individuals and organisations with whom he was having these so-called consultations. Truth be told, the decisions that were emanating from those consultations were being questioned by many church leaders, unionists, scientists, medical practitioners, educationists and businesspeople, to name but a few. If these organs of civil society were questioning the decisions, who was in consultation with who behind which closed doors?

In the meantime, regularly, at press briefings, every decision, the minister of health assured the nation, was driven primarily by a concern for the health and wellbeing of the people. This concern, as it seemed to appear to many disgruntled and impatient citizens, was an approach of COVID-19 above all else. One newspaper article in particular, suggested that virus fears were keeping HIV/Aids and TB patients from medication. According to the journalist, the drop in HIV/Aids and TB patients collecting their medication was due to transport restrictions and a fear on the part of patients being infected by the coronavirus.[94] In the same article, a survey by the organisation Right to Care and the Africa Health Research Institute (AHRI) revealed a decline of about 50%.

The other example of a crisis that was threatening the health and wellbeing of millions of South Africans was the problem of hunger. From the get go, after promises were made by government that the poorest households were going to receive either free groceries or a grocery voucher, the process was beset with all kinds of problems. These ranged from the identification of such households, to the logistics of sourcing and delivering the much needed food parcels to corrupt officials claiming the food parcels for themselves and then selling it to the poorest of the poor. In addition, those foot soldiers who were going out of their way to reach and feed the people were told that they were acting illegally.[95]

Businesses were closing their doors.[96] Not only because they were told to because of lockdown restrictions - but permanently. Many small and micro business owners were finding that they themselves were barely surviving. This would have a domino effect on the households whose breadwinners were employed by these businesses. The health and wellbeing of South Africa's citizens was indeed under threat, but not only by the coronavirus, but also by now it seemed, by the much greater threat of hunger and starvation. The slow process of getting the much-needed relief to the vulnerable households of the nation was not helping either. All these factors combined was becoming a very potent concoction that, if not brought under control, could explode.

I found it rather ironic and coincidental that the Sunday newspaper editor who was referring to 'the hour of the great storm' and this author was thinking along the same lines over the same weekend. In my online devotion[97] of Sunday, 17 May 2020, already recorded on Saturday, 16 May 2020, I was wondering aloud whether we should not consider the possibility that the South African nation was in the middle of a perfect storm. The lethal combination of huge uncertainty, growing frustration, rapidly increasing unemployment, more and more people going hungry, delayed and broken promises by government, a growing number of businesses in distress and individuals and groups threatening the government with court action seemed like the perfect ingredients for a perfect storm. The nation was waiting anxiously for the details of Level 3. Would wisdom prevail?

Chapter 26
LIVES VERSUS LIVELIHOODS

'...Oh, that you would choose life, so that you and
your descendants might live!'
Deuteronomy 30:19b (New Living Translation)

Difficult choices.

When the coronavirus and the killer disease that it carried, COVID-19 first made their appearance, right from the start, all over the globe, world leaders were all faced with extremely difficult choices. The same is true for the president of South Africa and his team of cabinet ministers and advisers who seemed determined to flatten the upward curve of the infection rate in South Africa. It came down to a choice between protecting the health of the nation versus protecting the economy of South Africa - it was not going to be possible to protect both at the same time. The president appeared to take decisive and calculated steps and within a matter of days, the citizens were locked down in their homes for an initial period of 21 days. It appeared the South African president was praised, from all over the world, for the manner in which he took leadership over the situation

But it was not long before it became clear that what was happening on the ground was not exactly a flattening of the curve at all, but in fact, quite the opposite. The infection rate and the death rate due to COVID-19 was steadily increasing and on more and more occasions, the nation had to hear that the worst was still to come. Depending who one was speaking to, projections were being made of a COVID-19 death toll of anything between 24 000 and 48 000[98] by November 2020. Moreover, in the city of Cape Town, the so-called epicentre of the disease in the country, in spite of the confidence of the premier that the province was ready for the worst, the situation seemed to be spiralling out of control. Almost two thirds of the country's confirmed cases ~~was~~ were in the Western Cape province and more specifically, in the Cape Metropolitan area.

While it seemed that the fight against the virus was far from won, on the economic front things were not looking too good either. Arguments were being raised on a number of fronts that all the effort to protect the health of the nation at the expense of the economy and people's livelihoods was not really delivering the expected results on the health side. Largely, the view of business was that the economy could be reopened to a significant extent while at the same making sure business was done safely.[99] The defence of the cabinet and the so-called Command Council on COVID-19 was simply that, if the measures were not introduced things would have turned out much worse[100] and the projected death toll would have been double than what was being predicted.

It was, of course, difficult to convince the thousands of suffering business owners and the millions of poor, unemployed and hungry South Africans that what they were going through could have been much worse. More and more ordinary South Africans started to question the government's alleged science versus common sense approach to handling the pandemic. In particular, the roundabout turns with the taxi and tobacco decisions. People justifiably wondered whether the original decisions were scientifically informed or whether the new decision to reverse the original was based on science or common sense. It seemed now, however noble and genuine the intentions of the Command Council on COVID-19 might have been in their handling of the pandemic, that in South Africa, a perfect storm was brewing.

When the president of the country addressed the nation for the second time within days of announcing that the country would be going down to alert Level 3 from Level 4 on the first day of June 2020, there was mixed reaction when he declared that religious gatherings might also resume as from 1 June 2020.[101] Even amongst themselves, church leaders seemed to be divided over the re-opening of church services. One the one hand, there were those who felt that the church was doing fine online and that it was an unnecessary risk exposing the faithful in such a manner, while others complained about the fact that not all church leaders were consulted. Others complained about only being allowed to preach to 50 people at a time.

It was this author's respectful observation that while some church leaders were now concerned about the safety of the flock within the four walls of the church, for weeks, even months, the same leaders were quite comfortable that their members were fairly safe travelling to work and to the shopping malls in a 70% filled minibus taxi.

Chapter 27
THE VIRUS IN SA – THINGS WE MAY NEVER KNOW

'The hidden things belong to the Lord our God,
but the revealed things belong to us…'
Deuteronomy 29:29a (Holman Christian Standard Bible)

As one of the South African cabinet ministers made it clear, 'we are working with science and not with common sense'. If that was the case, an explanation remains outstanding for many things. First and foremost (in the humble opinion of this author), how could it be safe to travel in a taxi filled to 70% capacity? In addition, if it was science which informed the initial decision to limit minibus taxi commuters to three per taxi, on what new science was the decision to backtrack based? In addition, how does one come to a scientific conclusion without asking specific questions and doing at least some research based on those questions? In the absence of questions and in the absence of common sense, then, we may never know whether the outbreaks in supermarkets and hospitals may be linked to staff who worked there and picked up the virus while commuting in a 70% filled taxi.

The second matter is the silence of the Church with regard to the very same taxi matter above. When one considers the 30-page document[102] prepared by the South African Council of Churches (SACC) and submitted for consideration to the Command Council on COVID-19, a genuine concern for the safety of God's flock may be discerned within those pages. It appeared that it was this concern for the safety of the faithful that prompted the Church leaders to deliver a document with such modest expectations like requesting permission from government to allow services of 50 people at a time in 500-seater and 1 000-seater and more facilities. The first unanswered question for this author is whether the Church leaders did not have a similar concern for taxi commuters? If indeed there had been such a concern, was the Church assuming a responsible posture by remaining silent about this matter?

The third aspect has to do with the level of what may have been perceived by some as selective law enforcement. From the first day of the initial period of lockdown, it became quite clear that life in most, if not all, of South Africa's townships would continue as it was before the lockdown. Long queues outside supermarkets and malls where no social distance was being maintained, crowds of people congregating everywhere almost on a daily basis and smoking and drinking continuing unabated. This was allowed by all the components of law enforcement that were supposed to be complementing each other in an effort to secure compliance with the lockdown rules and regulations. This, while thousands of others were being arrested for transgressing the lockdown regulations, including a young mom whose child had inadvertently walked from the road towards the beach.[103]

The fourth and final aspect that this author would like to highlight is the manner in which government responded when it became clear that the impact on the poor, in particular those in the most vulnerable households across the country, was proving to be the most devastating of all. Church leaders were already very much aware that online church was not really reaching the poorest church members, because the faithful did not have the same access to airtime and data as those more privileged South Africans who moved from a church in the building to an online church with relative ease. However, when the poor were told to apply online for the promised help from government, there was no audible, public objection that could be heard from within the ranks of the Church. The same silence on the part of the Church prevailed when government insisted that they would be the sole distributors of food parcels or food vouchers to the poor. Others had to go to court to fight against a government that was preventing them from feeding the poor.

In the 30-page submission of the South African Council of Churches to the Command Council on COVID-19 towards the end of May 2020, on page five there is a paragraph with the heading, 'Prophetic ministry at this time'. Under this heading, a number of important points are made. Amongst other, it is stated as follows, 'We cannot continue for too long under these lockdown restrictions and conditions. Many aspects of the rules promulgated by the Cabinet seemed to many of our people to be arbitrary and imposed without consultation. This is a danger to our society and weakens the social fabric of our nation, both for the present and for the future'. Perhaps a little too late, but well said. Moreover, what about the other matters raised by this author in this chapter?

Was it not the duty of the Church to respond to the arbitrariness of the decisions that were made? Was an injustice anywhere no longer an injustice everywhere? What may have been prevented had the voice of the Church been heard on those matters, not privately, behind closed doors, but publicly and audibly. Perhaps we may never know. Perhaps it is exactly this long silence of the Church that may be the reason why the cabinet was of the view that nothing similar would happen as had been the case with leaders in the taxi industry right at the outset of the lockdown rules. Because if you are quiet, it is much easier for others to send you to the back of the line and insist that you remain there until you receive further instructions.

Add to all of this, the fact that within your own ranks, there is division, with some declaring that they do not want to go back to church when it would be allowed to reopen its doors, then, an already weakened church, may potentially, be weakened even further.

Chapter 28
THE CHURCH – LAST IN LINE?

'Indeed there are those who are last who will be first,
and first who will be last.'
Luke 13:30 (New International Version)

All over the world, with very rare exceptions it seemed, the Church and the faithful would have to wait last in line for their turn to come. The common international practice, so it appeared, was to check what another country had done before you, then copy all or most of the lockdown restrictions locally. This would be described as applying best practice. In South Africa, one of the leading health experts, who was advising the South African government, openly declared that before they did anything, they would first ask China what they did.[104] So, one can imagine the sense of anticipation (even trepidation) while the South Africa nation was waiting with bated breath on their leader to come to the podium for the fourth time in almost as many months and explain the details of the next downward level (downward meant less restrictions) of Level 3.

Even more so, after what happened Down Under in mid-May did not bode well for the Church abroad. When New Zealand went down to Level 2, they introduced a number of measures that were supposed to be seen as a relaxing of the restrictions. There would be a distinction between what would be regarded as a public gathering and a private gathering. Attending a public event would include going to a conference, the cinema or the theatre, a stadium, casino or concert and at these types of events, 100 people at a time would be allowed to attend. The other category would be termed a private event or gathering and this category would include weddings, family events, religious services, parties at private households, group dinners (at

89

home or at a restaurant) and private functions like birthdays and funerals. A maximum of 10 people would be allowed to attend a private gathering, including church gatherings.[105]

About a week after these rules and regulations were announced in New Zealand, back in South Africa, national Church leaders made a submission to the government, which included proposals on how the Church should be allowed to regulate herself within the confines of defined restrictions when the nation would move from Level 4 to Level 3. When one regard the four corners of this 13-page submission (later 30 pages), the observant reader would very quickly discern that the expectations of the South African Church was, to say the least, modest. Amongst other, it seemed as if the Church was requesting that the limitations that were applying to the attendance of funerals on Levels 4 and 5 should also apply to other gatherings of the faithful under Level 3. Whether this modest approach could have been informed by the New Zealand experience is not known.

While this author understood, appreciated and respected the protocols, personally, I was not a huge supporter of, in my opinion, this way too modest approach. The protocols that I am referring to is the fact that my own denomination was a member of the body that made the submission and it was obvious that a number of different perspectives had to be accommodated in the submission. I was also aware that my own denomination had, weeks before the submission of the South African Council of Churches, made its own submission to the South African government. With the content of that submission, I was entirely comfortable and my national leaders were aware that their submission enjoyed my wholehearted support. Again, in my humble opinion, the level of expectation, even within the submission of the Apostolic Faith Mission (AFM) of South Africa, was still modest.[105]

I might have to concede that decision making under the circumstances that prevailed at the time, could not have been easy. For both the government and for the Church leaders who prepared the submissions referred to above. The death toll and the new number of confirmed cases of COVID-19 was rising daily in our country. In addition, the country's president and his team were already under constant attack from a number of quarters as various interest groups, as well as political parties, were threatening the government with court action. The country's rulers were also being lambasted for the perceived slowness in getting much needed relief to the poorest of the poor. An increasing number of businesses in distress were facing the reality of having to close their doors, which would leave thousands of households without an income.

Be that as it may. The Church is the Church - an institution that offers hope, help and healing. The spiritual, emotional, psychological and socio-economic effects of the extended period of lockdown on people was clearly proving to be devastating. To prevent people from having access to this critical source of support during such a time, by keeping the church doors shut, seemed, at the very least, to be counterproductive.

Chapter 29
THEY MET AT THE INTERSECTION

'...It is all decided by chance, by being in the
right place at the right time...'
Ecclesiastes 9:11 (New Living Translation)

We live in an imperfect world. A broken world.

This is evident in everything that is happening all around us. As the old hymn says, 'change and decay in everything we see'. For a long time each of us was trying to fix this brokenness on our own. The Church. The city. The government. Big business. Everybody else. Not because we were naive to believe that we could do it on our own, but because the collective effort is fraught with difficulty. The endeavour of bringing different stakeholders together around a table to discuss ways of finding solutions to common challenges, often bring with it even more challenges. Perspectives differ, priorities differ and intentions differ. In addition, all too often, the agendas and the desired outcomes that are being sought, also differ. That is how, after many failed attempts, we again end up on our own, trying to fix everything on our own.

History, they say, repeats itself. Again, this time, so it seemed, at least when fate and circumstance brought the Church, the politicians and the coronavirus crisis together at the intersection, another opportunity seemed to have been lost. In the first place, it became clear the first few times the president of South Africa took to the podium, that the Church was not high on the agenda. The Church, together with other religious organisations, was lumped with others under the heading of public gatherings. It appeared that, however long the period of so-called lockdown was going to be in place and whatever number of levels or stages it would take to open up the economy, the Church was meant to be last in line. Moreover, the Church, so it seemed, was willing to stand and wait there at the back of the queue, waiting like those destitute families for their promised food parcels, on the benevolence of the South African government.

During the last week of May, a 13-page document[106] (later 30 pages) prepared by the South African Council of Churches, was issued under the hand of its general secretary. My own denomination, the Apostolic Faith Mission of South Africa is a member of the SACC. It was a submission addressed to the president of South Africa and three cabinet ministers were copied into the correspondence. Briefly, it contains a submission by the Church where recommendations are made to the government on how the Church should be allowed to resume its activities, albeit in a much-reduced manner. The Church should be allowed to maintain its own supervision of the lockdown restrictions that may be applicable in the rules and regulations. I am not sure whether it is a fair observation on the part of this author, but I found it to be a little too late. It was now almost 60 days after the lockdown started.

It is this author's fervent prayer that he will not be misunderstood. I stand in full support of the president and government's approach to the COVID-19 crisis. The health and wellbeing of all South Africans is first, foremost and uppermost. On the part of the citizens, absolute compliance with all the rules of hygiene, social distancing and the wearing of masks is a non-negotiable necessity. A must. Whether at home, at work or on the way, full compliance with these rules is what will save the nation from certain disaster. On this point, there should be no ambiguity or double standards. It is exactly at this point of inconsistency where this author has difficulty reconciling himself with the positions of the government and national Church leaders. If a church member can travel to church safely in a 70% filled minibus taxi, why should they be limited to attend a service with only 49 of their fellow church members in a 500 seater building? What was the logic here? Why was it making sense to Church leaders? What was it that I was missing? This type of logic would have to be spoon-fed, very slowly, to this author.

Back in my city of Cape Town there was the example of the mayor[107] being accused (unfairly?) of trying to score political points for his party by using councillors to distribute food parcels to the poor and the destitute. Was the local churches and other institutions unwilling to assist? Were they approached at all? Someone wrote a book titled, *"We are smarter than Me"*. During this difficult time, it was this attitude that was required amongst leaders and their institutions. Right in the beginning of the lockdown period, we claimed that we were in this together,[108] but later the evidence seemed to prove otherwise. It is this author's humble view that, not too long from now, the Church should set aside some time for private reflection on how she was treated by other stakeholders during this time of crisis when the Church, under extremely difficult conditions, was making a difference in the lives of the poor in particular. Again, it seems, that the opportunity was not maximised when the Church, the city and the corona crisis met at the intersection. Hindsight might still reveal that a lot had to do with the posture that the Church herself assumed during the crisis.

94

Chapter 30
THE CONTINUED ROLE AND PRESENCE OF THE CHURCH

'He [Jesus] overturned the tables of the money
changers and the benches of those selling doves.'
Matthew 21:12 (New International Version)

As morbid as it may sound, about 150 000 people will die today.[109] The same will be true for tomorrow and the day after. In the midst of life we are in death, the saying goes. Some form of heart disease or cancer would have taken most of them, others through some or other respiratory disease. Yes, if the statisticians can be trusted, then more than 50 million people leave the planet every year to find their permanent resting place. When one considers the percentage of COVID-19 deaths compared to the total population per country, then a picture emerges that perhaps deserves more attention. Based on this percentage, according to the worst-case scenarios, a worldwide death toll of more than one and a half million[110] is expected and the countries that would be worst hit will probably be the US and Brazil.[111]

During the first five months of 2020, it appeared as if the world as we know it seemed to have found very little use for the Church of our Lord Jesus Christ. Even our presence and usefulness at funerals seemed to have diminished during the first months of the pandemic. Very limited attendance and rituals were allowed when only family and close friends turned up at the final goodbyes of those in the 150 000 who were not victims of the COVID-19 disease. On the other hand, in those instances where COVID-19 was indeed found to be the cause of death, very little, if any, religious rituals were allowed. Against the background of the highly infectious nature of the disease, this could probably be understood. However, with this author there remains a measure of unease when the value of the Church is so diminished that she is of little or no use, even during the final moments of her own members' time on earth.

I sincerely hope that this author's perception that the worldwide Church of our Lord Jesus Christ was opportunistically and deliberately sidelined by secular governments, will prove to be unfounded. That will make me feel so much better. However, if it may be found that this author was perhaps getting much closer to the truth than most imagined, then in all fairness to the decision makers who might be found to have deliberately sidelined the Church, the Church will herself (respectfully) not be able to walk away without taking some of the blame herself. Very often in life, it is not about stature, strength or speed, but about posture. The wise old Solomon teaches us that the fastest runner does not always win the race, and the strongest warrior does not always win the battle. The wise sometimes go hungry, and the skilful are not necessarily wealthy. Those who are educated do not always lead successful lives. Chance decides it all - by being in the right place at the right time.[112] Was the Church perhaps a victim of her own posture?

As mentioned in an earlier chapter, the leader of the movement did not leave the planet without giving instructions to his followers, a clear mandate - the creation and advancement of His Kingdom, right here on planet earth. According to this mandate, the disciples of Jesus (the Church) represent a movement on the go. A movement instructed and authorised to carry out the mandate of the Master, 'go, make disciples, baptise them and teach them to obey'. Our mandate is to build an empire, God's kingdom. An alternative society here on earth. That (in the author's humble view), should ideally be the posture of the Church of our Lord Jesus Christ here on earth. An empire-building movement, mandated and authorised by the One with all the power. The successful establishment of this alternative empire was supposed to make the world a better place.

However, when the monster called COVID-19 arrived on the planet, the Church was unceremoniously told to step aside, out of the way. The scientists and the politicians knew far better how to make the world a better place. The servants of the Church were not even found worthy of, at least, being declared essential workers. The flock could deal with the loss of income and hunger all on their own. Their government would take care of them. Food parcels would be delivered to their doors. Not by anyone. Not by the Church. Not by nonprofit organisations. Even if it would take a court case, government would be the hand of benevolence. The faithful could deal with the emotional and spiritual trauma caused by extended isolation and loss of livelihood all on their own. Because the Church (respectfully), it seemed, had assumed the posture of a beggar.

Chapter 31
A SEASON FOR LEADERSHIP

'If God has given you leadership ability,
take the responsibility seriously.'
Romans 12:8 (New Living Translation)

The impact of the coronavirus will be with us for the foreseeable future. The current season and the next will require leadership. As John Maxwell so aptly puts it, 'It rises and falls on leadership[113]'. Something about the end of the 22nd chapter of the Old Testament book of Ezekiel[114] has been fascinating me for a long time now. After God describes all the levels of leadership in the land (including the ordinary citizens) as being corrupt and untrustworthy, he still looks for a leader amongst them. The princes, the priests, the city officials, the prophets, as well as the people of the land are all guilty of violence, extortion, robbery and oppression. Why would God look for a leader amongst this crowd? Should one not go in search of a leader somewhere else that has a cleaner history? Is there perhaps a lesson in here somewhere that God is communicating to us about leadership selection?

Right through the Bible, it seems that God is always selecting what may appear as unlikely candidates. Moses stuttered, Jeremiah was too young, Peter was impulsive and Paul was a murderer. Rahab and Mary Magdalene were women of ill repute. The list goes on. God calls the unqualified and then qualifies them. He uses the so-called unwise to shame the wise of the world. Those who may disappoint God on their leadership journey are even given second chances. Think of David, Thomas, Peter and Paul. It seems that if God has decided to use someone, in the words of the poet, God drills, thrills, skills and moulds the person. God himself perfects whom he royally elects.

98

In my home country and over a significant part of the African continent (perhaps elsewhere) laws continue to be enacted with the church and church leaders as the target of the legislation. I am sure that there are those who will argue that church leaders themselves have invited this unwelcome attention. Accusations levelled against religious leaders range from staged miracles to the manipulative messages of progress and prosperity in return for bigger and bigger contributions to the coffers of the church. Very often, church leaders are accused of utilising church income to finance their own lavish lifestyles and to acquire assets for their own personal use and benefit. In addition, the faithful are encouraged to do strange things like drink fuel, eat grass and snakes and allow their leaders to spray them with insect killers.

These laws passed by political leaders are regrettable. Firstly, because, in the opinion of this author, the rules and regulations, arguably, are aimed at a very small, delinquent minority. Largely, church leaders live out their vocation under the most adverse conditions and receive very little financial reward in return. Pastors labour in under-resourced communities and have to contend with all the evils that are born from poverty, inequality and unemployment, amongst others crime, gangsterism, substance abuse, teenage pregnancy and a general lack of access to opportunities that are taken for granted in other contexts. In spite of the odds, these committed servant leaders report for duty every day. Secondly, not only Church leaders, but political leaders as well as business leaders are together responsible for the wellbeing of communities.

God is not looking for perfect people, but rather for those who, in spite of their imperfections, are moved into action when they refuse to accept that their cities and communities are doomed to a destiny of perpetual regression and hopelessness. God's servants are carriers and purveyors of hope. As one of the key leaders in our city would put it, if people have given up hope, then hope must find them. Church leaders are the bringers of this hope to our cities and our communities. Hope must find them through us. We should thank God for what, by His grace, we have already achieved, but there is still a lot to be done. It was such an encouragement to observe leadership in action when we could no longer sit back and do nothing about the suffering of our people during the devastation of the COVID-19 pandemic.

Mistakes were made. We all made mistakes. Politicians, business people, church leaders. We will continue to make mistakes. We are all products of the human race and we all have our flaws and imperfections. However, they say that the hottest places in hell are reserved for those who want to remain neutral and that evil triumphs when good people do nothing. We are also told that those who remain silent, when they ought to have spoken when they were able to do so, have agreed. As someone once said, 'the future does not come rolling in on the wheels of inevitability, but the future is shaped and determined by our efforts of today'. It is a season for leadership.

Chapter 32
LEADERS WHO MAKE A DIFFERENCE

'Those who are wise will shine as bright as the sky, and those who lead many to righteousness will shine like the stars forever.'
Daniel 12:3 (New Living Translation)

When the history of the novel coronavirus and the impact of COVID-19 on the world will be written, what, in hindsight, will be seen as the big picture? If a photographer captured the worldwide phenomenon as a range of images, which images will be visible to and which will not be? Which images will dominate and which will be difficult to discern? So often, we are reminded that we should focus on the big picture. Understandably so. Before the arrival of the coronavirus, there were already many challenges facing the global population and many of them already seemed insurmountable. When the COVID-19 pandemic arrived, the trajectory of the world's problems was dramatically altered. The learning curve was probably even steeper than the planet's attempts to flatten the upward curve of infection and death of COVID-19.

When one reflects on current world challenges, given the conditions and their complexities, who can really make a difference? Inequality, poverty, unemployment, climate change, urbanisation. The list seems endless. Every year, world leaders meet to discuss possible solutions to these problems and every year they emerge with ideas that do not really inspire or convince the people most affected by these global challenges. Perhaps the answer to this question, who can make a difference, lies in the same answer to the other question, how does one eat an elephant? The smart answer, of course, is piece by piece. Perhaps we should take courage when, in small corners, all over the world there are unsung heroes and wonderful servants of both God

101

and humanity who continue, on a daily basis, to make a difference in the lives of the people around them, right where they are.

The difference that these leaders make in the lives of ordinary people often goes by unnoticed and unappreciated. On a daily basis, they have to spend their time and energy serving desperate and needy people. Much is asked of these leaders and they continue to give willingly of themselves and of their time. Yet as is often the case, they receive very little in return. Nevertheless, during this pandemic, as could be observed on the streets of our cities around the world, they still soldier on and continue to make a difference, in spite of everything. It is often assumed that it is only words that these leaders have to offer, only prayers and words of encouragement and hope. That their contribution is limited to Sunday sermons, weddings and funerals. However, the truth is that the people that they lead expect much more from them. Often they are approached for direction and advice beyond the scope of their training and vocation.

Every time they go beyond the call of duty, they find themselves, like our Lord Jesus Christ himself, in the strangest of places amongst the strangest of characters. Amongst others, often ending up mediating in gang violence, accompanying abused persons to police stations, sitting long hours in courts in support of those in their care and, on a regular basis, finding themselves having to mediate between the powerful and the vulnerable. Observing these servant leaders taking to the streets at the height of the pandemic and at risk of breaching lockdown rules in their efforts to relieve the plight of the poor, brought a tear to my eye on more than one occasion. Having very little or nothing themselves, they gave everything.

A year or more before the coronavirus came along and changed everything, there was much publicity focused on the few opportunists, charlatans and wannabes who had entered the space where these heroes live out their vocation and calling. As it appears sometimes in the process, everyone is tarnished with the same brush. The few who exploit poor and innocent people are highlighted in the media, at the expense of all. Leaders are, of course like other humans, not without their flaws and imperfections, but those who do an honest day's work, every day, over a lifetime, deserve acknowledgment, appreciation and honour, not the disrespect and disdain often meted out to them. As could be seen when the hour came, they do make a difference.

It is my hope and prayer that these amazing individuals will not lose heart, but continue to do what governments and businesses (respectfully) on their own, are seemingly unable to do. I thank God for having blessed me with the grace and good fortune to have worked with and continue to work with hundreds, perhaps thousands, of these life changing individuals and to have, over time, witnessed the impact and difference that they make in the lives of the people that they have touched. Always ready, always willing, always available. I have written this book, first for the benefit of leaders. Primarily those leaders who lead churches and other nonprofit organisations. More specifically, for those leaders who lead under-resourced organisations in under-resourced communities, but who, in spite of the odds against them, continue to make a difference. However, I also hope that this book has been and will be read by persons from all other walks of life and across generations. In fact, I would be extremely humbled if that turns out to be the case.

Chapter 33
LIFE AFTER LOCKDOWN – WHERE TO START?

'They replied, "Let us start rebuilding." So they began this good work.'
Nehemiah 2:18 (New International Version)

There is an old saying, 'sweep in front of your own door' and there is an old chorus that suggests we should 'brighten the corner where we are'. When one considers the rebuilding process in the third book of the prophet Nehemiah,[115] one comes across repeated references to 'each one in front of his own house' and 'opposite his house' and so on. The rebuilding process always starts with one individual, in his or her own space. Even now, months after the imprisonment of lockdown, one's own house might have become a different space or a strange space. The exiles in Babylon, far from home, filled with longing for their old, familiar surroundings received a similar instruction from God through the prophet Jeremiah.[116]

'Work towards the peace and prosperity of the city where you are', they were told. They were encouraged to get involved in the economy of Babylon, to settle down and acquire property. Instructions were given to plant their own gardens and live from the produce thereof. Inspired to plan generationally, God was directing their gaze and vision towards the future. After giving them instructions to work, produce and multiply, then, and only then, were they also instructed to pray. Perhaps, this will be the new order of business after lockdown, less talk, more walk and getting down to the task of rebuilding.

The new habits that will be required for the new life after lockdown should have been practised since the first day of lockdown. Noncompliance was and is not an option. We have to develop and maintain new routines as far as our personal hygiene and keeping a safe social distance is concerned. If the wearing of masks will offer protection against infection, let us wear them. Let us decontaminate surfaces and devices on a regular basis. At home. At work. At church. At play. Let us leave no stone unturned in our efforts to leave a better place behind for those generations who come after us.

Church leaders will have to set the example. Even when church activities are allowed to continue on an increasing scale, it will certainly come with many restrictions. If our facilities may be filled to only 25% capacity, let us comply and reimagine new ways of doing church. The faithful will have to learn the disciplines of living without the hug and the handshake and appreciate the wave of the hand and touch of the elbow. We should call out those charlatans and opportunists who have crept in through the windows. We may never know what portion of the blame can be placed on the conduct of these individuals for the treatment that the Church received from government during the period of lockdown. Nevertheless, it can no longer be business as usual.

Yes. We should continue to pray. Pray more earnestly. Besides praying there is much work to do. It is time to roll up our sleeves and get our hands dirty. There has been a lot of devastation. Unemployment has increased exponentially leaving breadwinners and their families destitute. Households that were already vulnerable before the lockdown restrictions, find themselves in a crisis. Small and micro business owners have been left without income and livelihood for weeks, even months, and are not sure about whether they will be able to rebuild their businesses successfully. Their staff are in an even worse position.

In all of this rebuilding, the Church should not underestimate the role it can and must play. When the parents of the young Jesus found him teaching in the temple after searching for him for days and enquired of Him why he would do such a thing to them, His response to His parents was a question, 'Did you not know that I must be about my Father's business?[117]' All of this is our Father's business. Seeking the lost, the wounded and the broken. Offering them hope and faith in a better future. Finding the hurt and healing it, finding the need, and as far as it is within our means, filling it. The work awaits. Let us rise and rebuild.

Where was the Church? She was there. In the streets. Where the pain was. Where the brokenness was. Where the hunger was. Sometimes she was even found online, as they say.

She was seen. Her hands and feet of love, care and compassion was seen and felt everywhere.

However, was she really heard? Did she really say what was needed to be said?

AFTERWORD

'The end of a matter is better than its beginning...'
Ecclesiastes 7:8a (New International Version)

When will it end? How will it end?

New epicentres emerge. The coronavirus continues to move from epicentre to epicentre. At the time of writing, Brazil had overtaken the United States (US) as far as the daily death rate was concerned.[118] On 31 May 2020, there were more than 6 million confirmed cases of infected people in the world with more than 370 000 deaths. More than 70% of those deaths occurred amongst the six countries of the United States, United Kingdom, Italy, Brazil, Spain and France. It is predicted that this year alone, the coronavirus and the disease that it carries, COVID-19, will add another million or two to the 50 million annual deaths amongst global citizens. Perhaps more questions than answers will remain. When it ends and how it ends might perhaps prove to be less important questions than the question - are we ready and willing to remember what we have learned and apply these lessons in the continued work of building a future for the coming generations?

Some might have more work to do than others might. There are places on the planet where the devastation has come at an extremely high cost. It is projected that in a worst-case scenario, over the next few months, between countries like Brazil, the US, the UK, Mexico and India a combined total of almost one and half million souls might succumb to the COVID-19 disease. The urban centres in these countries will probably emerge from the coronavirus crisis with the highest number of casualties. The challenges facing the world's cities, which have been briefly highlighted in this work, will have a new

107

dimension added as the world braces itself for similar types of outbreaks in the future. These challenges facing global cities also present a challenge to the Church to find new ways of making a meaningful contribution in her efforts to add value to the lives of these citizens.

In spite of the attempted sideline by governments across the globe, the Church and her servants could not stand idly by with so much devastation and suffering all around her. The Church could be seen almost everywhere where there was hunger, pain and brokenness. Even while her own servants were facing similar circumstances in their own local churches and homes, from their own modest resources they shared with those who were less fortunate than they were. As God's own hands and feet, the Church was there for the poor, the widow, the orphan and the stranger. Reaching out, caring, comforting, clothing and bringing desperately needed relief where it was most required. In the cities of the world, there will always be a place and a role for the Church. In our collective future, greater collaboration between the Church, the cities of the world, the world's governments and the business fraternity is inevitable.

I write these words on 31 May 2020 or Pentecost Sunday, as it would be called on the calendar of the Church. It was on this day, those many years ago when the leaders of the Church were probably hiding away in the upper room for fear of arrest and prosecution, when their escape from the upper room and their fearless entry onto the streets of the Roman Empire was made possible by an intervention from God himself. Arguably, this time it could be said that the Church unwittingly escaped from the potential entrapment of her own four walls, aided by those who believed that they had been called to deal with the onslaught of the coronavirus without the help of the Church. Perhaps now, with hindsight, the Church is right where she belongs, at large, at liberty, not yet captured. Will she use this newfound freedom to, once again, be the instrument in God's hand that ushers in the revival of the new Pentecost as we begin our work afresh and anew in the cities and towns of the world?

The God given mandate to the human race is to be fruitful and productive, to replenish, subdue and have dominion on the planet. God has placed the privilege and burden of stewardship on the human race. Moreover, as Paul reminds us, it is required of stewards that they be found faithful.[119] Time will probably be the judge of the quality of management and stewardship that prevailed during the crisis that was brought upon humanity by the coronavirus and COVID-19. As the words of the song of Steve Green implore us, 'may all who come behind us find us faithful.'

When will it end? How will it end? If all of us stay the course and we all continue to do what must be done, it may still all end well.

DETAILS, DEFINITIONS AND EXPLANATIONS OF KEY TERMS

1. *Artificial Intelligence* - the theory and development of computer systems able to perform tasks normally requiring human intelligence, such as visual perception, speech recognition, decision making and translation between languages.

2. *Barna Group* - www.barna.com

3. *Church The* - The word Church is capitalised when it refers to the body of Christians who comprise Christ's Church and when it is part of the proper name of a church.

4. *church* - Church in lowercase refers to any local church, anywhere in the world.

5. *church online* - an expression used when church services are delivered from an online platform.

6. *church at home* - an expression used when church services are delivered from an online platform and members are viewing at home.

7. *Church at large* - that part of the Church that is still at liberty (free) to carry out her Biblical mandate, un-captured by politicians, donors, academics or any other interested party.

8. *City* - an urban centre experiencing a continuous influx of people from rural areas or areas where there are less opportunities to make a decent living.

9. *Confirmed cases* - any person meeting the laboratory criteria where there is detection of SARS-CoV-2 nucleic acid in a clinical specimen.

10. *Consulta* - www.consulta.co.za

11. *Epicentre* - the central point of something, typically a difficult or unpleasant situation.

12. *Fourth Industrial Revolution* - The fourth industrial revolution is the current and developing environment in which disruptive technologies and trends such as artificial intelligence and other digital realities are changing the way we live and work.

13. *Inclusiveness* - the practice or policy of including people who might otherwise be excluded or marginalised, such as those who have physical or mental disabilities and members of minority groups.

14. *Informal settlement* - areas where groups of housing units have been constructed on land that the occupants have no legal claim to, or occupy illegally; ... unplanned settlements and areas where housing is not in compliance with current planning and building regulations (unauthorised housing).

15. *Leadership* - leadership is the art of motivating a group of people to act towards achieving a common goal.

16. *Mampara* - in South Africa, a derogatory term referring to a person lacking intelligence or sense.

111

17. *Millennials* - a person reaching young adulthood in the early 21st century.

18. *movement.org* - New York based organisation

19. *Novel coronavirus* - Coronavirus disease 2019 (COVID-19) is defined as an illness caused by a novel coronavirus now called severe acute respiratory syndrome coronavirus 2 (SARS-CoV-2; formerly called 2019-nCoV)

20. *Pew Research Centre* - www.pewresearch.org

21. *Posture* - a particular approach or attitude.

22. *Slum* - a squalid and overcrowded urban street or district inhabited by very poor people (often in the inner city).

23. *Sustainable development* - economic development that is conducted without depletion of natural resources.

24. *Teen Challenge* - www.teenchallengeusa.org

25. *Township* - (in South Africa) a suburb or city of predominantly black occupation, formerly officially designated for black occupation *by apartheid legislation.*

LIST OF SOURCES AND WEB LINKS

1. Green, Steve. 'O, may all who come behind us find faithful.' 1988.

2. Herbert, Trevor. 1994. *Affirmative Action in the South African Workplace.*

3. Fisher, Dale. 2020 Video. https://www.youtube.com/watch?v=VSQnOS7t4Gg

4. https://www.samrc.ac.za/news/what-we-think-we-know-about-covid-19-epidemiological-numbers

5. https://en.wikipedia.org/wiki/List_of_global_issues

6. https://en.wikipedia.org/wiki/Cape_Town_water_crisis

7. https://www.dailymail.co.uk/news/article-8287645/Frenchman-43-reveals-patient-zero-coronavirus-December.html

8. https://www.thelocal.se/20200505/the-coronavirus-may-have-arrived-in-sweden-in-november

9. https://www.who.int/dg/speeches/detail/who-director-general-s-remarks-at-the-media-briefing-on-2019-ncov-on-11-february-2020

10. https://www.worldometers.info/coronavirus/country/china/

11. https://en.wikipedia.org/wiki/COVID-19_pandemic_in_Italy

12.   https://en.wikipedia.org/wiki/COVID-19_pandemic_in_Spain

13.   https://en.wikipedia.org/wiki/
       COVID-19_pandemic_in_the_United_States

14.   https://en.wikipedia.org/wiki/
       COVID-19_pandemic_in_South_Africa

15.   Weekend Argus, 21 March, Front page

16.   https://www.channel24.co.za/Music/News/large-gatherings-of-
       more-than-100-people-temporarily-prohibited-in-south-
       africa-20200315

17.   Cape Times, 24 March, 2020, Front Page

18.   City Press, 26 April 2020, Front Page

19.   https://www.nortonrosefulbright.com/en/knowledge/
       publications/10fb417c/sa-moves-to-level4-covid19-lockdown

20.   https://www.timeslive.co.za/sunday-times/opinion-and-
       analysis/2020-05-31-how-cyril-went-from-secular-saint-to-
       mampara/

21.   Sunday Times, 29 March 2020, Front Page

22.   Sunday Times 19 April 2020, Front Page

23.   City Press, 19 April 2020, Front Page

24. Cape Argus 15 April 2020, Front Page

25. City Press, 26 April 2020, Front Page

26. Labour Minister Thulas Nxesi, 3 May 2020, Press briefing

27. https://www.sanews.gov.za/south-africa/transport-revises-taxi-regulations-during-lockdown

28. https://www.news24.com/news24/southafrica/news/lockdown-fresh-court-challenge-likely-after-govt-backtracks-on-lifting-cigarette-sales-ban-20200430

29. https://ewn.co.za/2020/05/03/ancwl-attack-on-dlamini-zuma-over-tobacco-ban-aims-to-pit-her-against-ramaphosa

30. https://www.news24.com/news24/southafrica/news/bizarre-and-irregular-british-american-tobacco-on-governments-tobacco-ban-20200501

31. https://ewn.co.za/2020/04/30/mboweni-i-lost-the-debate-on-alcohol-and-cigarette-sales

32. https://www.dailymaverick.co.za/article/2020-05-11-trevor-manuel-sas-lockdown-rules-do-not-pass-test-of-rationality/

33. https://www.gov.za/speeches/president-cyril-ramaphosa-south-africas-response-coronavirus-covid-19-pandemic-13-may-2020

34. https://www.channel24.co.za/Music/News/large-gatherings-of-more-than-100-people-temporarily-prohibited-in-south-africa-20200315

35. https://www.news24.com/news24/southafrica/news/acdp-leader-kenneth-meshoe-pastor-angus-buchan-among-those-exposed-to-covid-19-positive-tourists-report-20200322

36. https://www.dispatchlive.co.za/news/opinion/2017-09-30-drawing-the-very-fine-line-between-church-and-state/

37. Proverbs 24:10

38. 1 Timothy 5:8

39. https://www.news24.com/citypress/Voices/thabo-makgoba-virus-unites-all-of-gods-children-20200412

40. https://citizen.co.za/parenty/2270703/watch-prof-jansen-says-scrap-entire-2020-school-year-pass-all-students/

41. Sunday Times, 31 May 2020, Page 5

42. Cape Argus 23 April 2020, Front Page

43. City Press, 19 April 2020, Front Page

44. Constitution of the Western Cape Ecumenical Network

45. Luke 9:22

46. John 10:18

47. Matthew 16:10

48. Hybels, Bill 2002, *Courageous Leadership*
49. Matthew 6:3

50. https://www.iol.co.za/pretoria-news/allegations-to-stop-non-profit-organisations-from-distributing-food-false-lindiwe-zulu-48076023

51. https://www.news24.com/news24/southafrica/news/lockdown-here-are-the-guidelines-to-donate-or-deliver-food-parcels-in-gauteng-20200519

52. Matthew 28:19-20

53. https://static1.squarespace.com/static/568afc205a56689beca7dba1/t/56cb308907eaa09d5d4a066c/1456156813914/ASDM+Brochure.pdf

54. https://thelastwell.org/the-current-state-of-christianity-in-africa/

55. Matthew 5:13-14

56. Matthew v13:31-32

57. https://www.politicsweb.co.za/opinion/we-must-eliminate-the-evil-triplets--susan-shabang

58. https://www.macrotrends.net/cities/22481/cape-town/population

59. https://www.capetownetc.com/news/cape-town-the-worlds-11th-most-dangerous-city/

60. https://www.htxt.co.za/2014/01/15/new-york-times-names-cape-town-best-place-visit-2014/

61. https://www.capetown.travel/cape-town-voted-best-city-in-the-world-for-7th-year-running/

62. https://www.washingtonpost.com/world/africa/south-africa-coronavirus-cape-town-superspreader/2020/05/18/4d332248-9566-11ea-87a3-22d324235636_story.html

63. Cape Times 30 March 2020, Front Page

64. https://www.talkofthetown.co.za/2020/05/13/sas-big-cities-and-coronavirus-hotspots-could-remain-under-level-4/

65. https://www.news24.com/news24/southafrica/news/western-cape-bracing-for-estimated-80-000-covid-19-cases-20200421

66. https://www.iol.co.za/news/south-africa/western-cape/105-tygerberg-hospital-staff-test-positive-for-covid-19-48330664

67. https://www.sowetanlive.co.za/news/south-africa/2020-04-22-western-cape-covid-19-infections-pass-1000-and-deaths-rise-to-22/

68. Cape Times, 9 Aril 2020, Front page

69. Cape Times, 20 April 2020, Front age

70. https://www.iol.co.za/capeargus/news/watch-strandfontein-homeless-shelter-described-as-a-concentration-camp-46502470

71. Cape Times, 16 April 2020, Front page

72. https://accountingweekly.com/the-court-cases-begin-now-cigarette-makers-taking-government-to-court-over-ban/

73. https://www.sanews.gov.za/south-africa/department-announces-details-relief-fund-athletes-artists

74. John 3:16

75. https://www.nationalgeographic.com/news/2018/02/cape-town-running-out-of-water-drought-taps-shutoff-other-cities/

76. https://ourworldindata.org/urbanization

77. https://www.theguardian.com/news/datablog/2009/aug/18/percentage-population-living-cities

78. Alvin Toffler (1928-2016)

79. Malachi 3:10

80. Romans 15:1

81. https://www.bbc.com/news/world-africa-52323375

82. https://thelastwell.org/the-current-state-of-christianity-in-africa/

83.   https://www.weforum.org/agenda/2018/06/Africa-urbanization-cities-double-population-2050-4%20ways-thrive/

84.   https://365prophetic.com/th/2019/01/19/2019-prophecies-over-africa-korea-and-other-nations/

85.   http://www.scielo.org.za/scielo.php?script=sci_arttext&pid=S1017-04992018000100014

86.   https://www.africanews.com/2020/06/03/coronavirus-in-africa-breakdown-of-infected-virus-free-countries/

87.   https://www.worldometers.info/coronavirus/country/madagascar/

88.   https://english.alarabiya.net/en/coronavirus/2020/05/11/Madagascar-coronavirus-medicine-scorned-because-it-s-from-Africa-says-President

89.   https://twitter.com/DrZweliMkhize/status/1257952610461646848

90.   https://mg.co.za/africa/2020-05-11-question-marks-surround-madagascars-covid-19-miracle-cure/

91.   https://www.dailymaverick.co.za/article/2020-05-11-trevor-manuel-sas-lockdown-rules-do-not-pass-test-of-rationality/#gsc.tab=0

92.   https://www.bloomberg.com/news/articles/2020-05-07/south-african-business-wants-virus-lockdown-ended-within-weeks

93.   https://www.pressreader.com/south-africa/sunday-
        times-1107/20200517/281994674679795

94.   https://www.timeslive.co.za/sunday-times/news/2020-05-17-
        coronavirus-fears-keep-hiv-tb-patients-from-medication/

95.   https://www.dailymaverick.co.za/article/2020-05-05-how-red-
        tape-is-hampering-the-hungry-from-receiving-food-in-south-
        africa/

96.   https://www.fin24.com/Opinion/sa-businesses-are-shutting-
        down-at-an-alarming-rate-and-we-need-urgent-reforms-to-
        turn-the-tide-20190614-2

97.   Facebook post, 17 May 2020, facebook.com/afmeersteriver

98.   https://mg.co.za/coronavirus-essentials/2020-05-20-south-
        africa-could-see-40-000-covid-19-deaths-by-november/

99.   Business Times, 24 May 2020, Front page

100.   Statement, President Ramaphosa, 13 May 2020

101.   https://ewn.co.za/2020/05/24/level-3-all-the-lockdown-
        regulation-changes-come-1-june

102.   SACC - 30 Page submission to Command Council on Covid
        19

103.   https://www.news24.com/news24/southafrica/news/lockdown-
        cape-town-parents-bad-nightmare-after-arrest-for-fetching-
        toddler-who-wandered-onto-beach-20200505

104.   https://www.youtube.com/watch?v=OQ8qb7eGS8c

105.   https://www.stuff.co.nz/national/health/coronavirus/
121608507/church-leaders-call-for-gathering-limits-to-be-
raised-to-100-people

106.   AFM of SA submission to Command Council on Covid 19

107.   SACC 13 Page Draft Document

108.   https://www.iol.co.za/capetimes/news/call-for-dan-platos-
head-for-violating-directive-on-distributing-food-48118257

109.   Cape Argus 16 March 2020, Front Page

110.   https://www.weforum.org/agenda/2020/05/how-many-people-
die-each-day-covid-19-coronavirus

111.   https://www.news24.com/news24/World/News/coronavirus-
how-many-people-will-die-it-could-be-millions-20200319

112.   https://www.worldometers.info/coronavirus/

113.   Ecclesiastes 9:11 (New Living Translation)

114.   Maxwell, John. 2007, The 21 Irrefutable laws of leadership

115.   Ezekiel 22: 25-30

116.   Nehemiah 3

117. Jeremiah 29:7

118. Luke 2:49

119. https://www.khaosodenglish.com/news/international/
2020/05/26/brazil-overtakes-u-s-in-worst-one-day-death-toll-
from-covid-19/

120. 1 Corinthians 4:2

THE CHURCH, THE CITY & THE VIRUS

COMMENTS BY MG MAHLOBO
PRESIDENT: THE APOSTOLIC FAITH MISSION OF SOUTH AFRICA

1. Let me start by expressing appreciation and thanks to Trevor for inviting me to make a comment or review on this, his second book.

2. Trevor's views on what he refers to, as the silence of the church, on the treatment it received from Government, during the state of national disaster and lockdown is well articulated in this book.

3. His analysis on the coronavirus outbreak to the point where it was declared a global pandemic, must be applauded. I am of the view that it is based on credible primary sources. Furthermore, it has demonstrated that he is not just an avid reader but also a critical analytic. In his critique he maintains his respect for church leadership.

4. One must, from the onset, state that this pandemic caught many of us off guard. It has all the key elements of a crisis.

    a. Like all pandemics Covid-19 had, the threat-element, the surprise-element, and the urgency-element (decisions had to be made quickly).
    b. The other element to the Covid-19 pandemic is the high level of uncertainty. This is despite reliance on science and projections that are made from time to time.

124

c. All of us, including Government and Churches were caught up in a pandemic that ambushed our schedules, had a potential of overwhelming our health facilities, threaten the lives and livelihood of our people.

d. The Coronavirus is correctly characterised as a corona crisis because of its uniqueness and its potential to overwhelm all available resources.

Some issues raised by the Author

5. It seems his critique is sparked by the following:

a. The church's response was not heard when the church's meetings were restricted to 100 per site prior to the national lockdown.

b. The church's voice was not heard when its gatherings were prohibited under the national lockdown, now referred to as Alert level 5.

c. Furthermore, the church's silence was conspicuous when taxis were allowed 70% of passenger occupancy while the church buildings remained locked.

d. The silence of the church on the distribution of the R500 billion Relief Fund.

e. He strongly feels that the church should have raised an alarm when the Government issued conflicting message regarding the sale of tobacco.

6. I may, have missed other critical issues that he is raising, due to time constraints. For this reason, I would like to confine myself to the ones I have mentioned.

125

7.   The author correctly points out that the President of the country was in an invidious position. But the church also found itself in an unpleasant situation. In such a situation, leaders are likely to take decisions that may cause resentment. On the other hand , failure to take a decision is not a choice.

8.   Let me take issue with the concept of "silence". The author did not provide any glossary to assist me understand his understanding of the concept. Silence on the part of the church is subject to various interpretations.

    a.   One of the quotes ascribed to Mahatma Ghandi is: "Silence becomes cowardice when occasion demands speaking out the whole truth and acting accordingly."
    b.   The other quote that might be relevant to this situation is "The ultimate tragedy is not the oppression and cruelty by the bad people but the silence over that by the good people" (Dr Martin Luther King Jr).
    c.   It does not seem the author has any of the two quotes in mind when he refers to the silence of the church (Chapter 7).

9.   My view is that the church's response should not be judged on what it did not say but rather on what it failed to do in mitigating the pandemic spread.

10.   Unfortunately, the author seems to rely on one document of the Church leaders belonging to the South African Council of Churches National Leaders Forum (SACC NCLF) namely the policy document on Covid-19 Norms and Standards.

126

11. Prior to this policy document the SACC NCLF produced a Pastoral Plan to mitigate the effects of the pandemic. The principles guiding this Pastoral Plan were:

   a. Respect the integrity and the purpose of the lockdown such that our process of giving food to people who are desperately hungry, does not become a vehicle of the spread of the disease and thus inadvertently cause death amongst the most vulnerable in society.

   b. Ensure that we do not create a situation where our people are part of a stampede in a desperate attempt to get food parcels which they believe might run out before they get theirs. This might result in ugly scenes and possible injuries.

   c. Ensure that every part of the country where the people are, is reached at the same time in real time, and avoid the possibility of those in the cities being advantaged while those who are in the remote areas are excluded or considered last.

   d. Protect and respect the dignity of our people in their state of need.

   e. Mitigate if not totally eliminate, the scope of corruption.

   f. Keep alive the local commercial infrastructure of neighbourhoods, regular shops and spazas.

12. If the question is: "Did the church do enough within its power to drive the pandemic down?" My answer would be yes and no.

a. The answer is in the affirmative when one considers the sacrifices made by the church when it cancelled its Good Friday Conferences and other events. The fact that church buildings were closed for five weeks was a huge sacrifice on the part of the church.

b. However, the church did not raise its voice in time and sufficiently for pastors to be part of the essential services.

c. The church did not raise its voice against the rationality of the Alert Level 4 Regulations. We should have done this. On this one I agree with the author's view.

13. Let me come other instances where, according to the author, the church was silent.

14. The author raises the silence on the part of the church with reference to taxis being allowed to have 70% passenger occupancy.

a. What the author fails to appreciate is that passenger activities in a taxi are different from the activities of church members in the church building.

b. The other issue that placed the church in a precarious position was patient 31 in South Korea whose infection led to the infection many people in Korea. The fact that the church became an epicentre of infection in Korea was not something that could be ignored.

c. The infections in the Bloemfontein church conference which almost had similar effect on fellow South Africans could not be brushed aside as a non-issue.

15. The next issue relates to the silence of the church on the question of Alert Level 4 irrational laws.

    a.   Indeed our church did not challenge the national lockdown. The church had taken a posture of compliance.

    b.   On the issue of irrationality of the Covid-19 Regulations, our own church leadership secured a legal opinion on this matter.

    c.   We then took a particular strategy to raise this matter with Government and only approach the Courts of the land if this attempt failed.

    d.   When church gatherings were allowed under Alert level 3 and pastors' essential service was acknowledged our strategy was not taken further because Alert Level 3 eased restrictions on church gatherings and accommodated pastors as part of the essential service.

16. The other issue where the author's church is taken to task in the book is the distribution of the 500 Billion Rand Relief Fund.

    a.   It is not clear to me whether the author is alleging that Government could not be trusted in ensuring that this money is distributed fairly.

    b.   I am not sure whether the church did have evidence of corruption in this regard.

    c.   If, however, it can be proven that the church did nothing in the face of evidence of corruption, in this regard, then the church is guilty on this one.

d.	I must, however, emphasise, that it would be dangerous for the church to take action in the absence of evidence.

17.	The church, as part of the community, has been adversely affected by the coronavirus. We must all find ways of dealing with the impact of the pandemic on the life and operations of the church. In this regard the author is spot on when he speaks of difficult choices between lives and livelihoods (Chapter 26).

18.	I must also differ with the author when he avers that the church was told to step aside.

a.	The lockdown did not amount to censoring the ministry of the church.
b.	The church's ministry is not confined to church buildings.
c.	The dominant view on the church's side was that church members should not become virus transmitters but hope transmitters.

19.	I would like to conclude by saluting Trevor for the manner in which he was able to put on paper his views. I am convinced that this book will trigger deep reflection on what the church should have done.

Thank you, Trevor. God bless you!

Introduction

The evil twins. Covid 19 and Inequality.

The one arrived long before the other. But when the second showed up on the scene the first was exposed in all its nakedness. All over the planet, wherever the second twin planted its devastating footprints the other was revealed in all the same kinds of places where similar living conditions prevailed. Wherever there was poverty the twins left a trail of suffering and devastation. It seemed that the threat to food security would overwhelm the dangers that presented themselves as far as the health of the world's poorest communities was concerned.

Year after year, ironically, in one of the richest countries in the world, global leaders reflect on the common challenges that face humanity. At the top of that list of challenges would be inequality, poverty and unemployment. Imagine the scene - the business and political elite gather in one of the wealthiest corners of the globe to talk about extreme poverty and the growing gap between the haves and the have nots. As someone once remarked, *"over expensive steaks in luxury hotels they discuss the problem of world hunger"*. And every time they seem to emerge with the "poorest" solutions!

132

ABOUT THE AUTHOR

Trevor Herbert is a former senior executive in the retail sector who opted for full-time pastoral ministry in the year 2000. Currently he serves as a pastor in the Apostolic Faith Mission of South Africa (AFM of SA), one of the larger denominations in South Africa (1.4 million members). The AFM of SA has a footprint in Africa, Asia and Australia as well as parts of Europe and the USA.

Trevor is also involved in a number of city and community impacting organisations as well as local and global ecumenical initiatives. He lives in Cape Town, South Africa and is a father of three children, two sons-in-law and grandfather of two grandsons. He is married to Moira (a retired nurse) for 37 years. The family resides in the northern suburbs of Cape Town. This is his second book after his first work, *Affirmative Action in the South African Workplace* was published in 1994.

First print June 2020